Richard Purdie, Chris Larson, and Phil Blundell, BitBake
Community **<bitbake-devel@lists.openembedded.org>**

by Richard Purdie, Chris Larson, and Phil Blundell
Copyright © 2004-2016 Richard Purdie, Chris Larson, and Phil Blundell

Table of Contents

Chapter 1. Overview

Welcome to the BitBake User Manual. This manual provides information on the BitBake tool. The information attempts to be as independent as possible regarding systems that use BitBake, such as OpenEmbedded and the Yocto Project. In some cases, scenarios or examples within the context of a build system are used in the manual to help with understanding. For these cases, the manual clearly states the context.

1.1. Introduction

Fundamentally, BitBake is a generic task execution engine that allows shell and Python tasks to be run efficiently and in parallel while working within complex inter-task dependency constraints. One of BitBake's main users, OpenEmbedded, takes this core and builds embedded Linux software stacks using a task-oriented approach.

Conceptually, BitBake is similar to GNU Make in some regards but has significant differences:

* BitBake executes tasks according to provided metadata that builds up the tasks. Metadata is stored in recipe (.bb) and related recipe "append" (.bbappend) files, configuration (.conf) and underlying include (.inc) files, and in class (.bbclass) files. The metadata provides BitBake with instructions on what tasks to run and the dependencies between those tasks.

* BitBake includes a fetcher library for obtaining source code from various places such as local files, source control systems, or websites.

* The instructions for each unit to be built (e.g. a piece of software) are known as "recipe" files and contain all the information about the unit (dependencies, source file locations, checksums, description and so on).

* BitBake includes a client/server abstraction and can be used from a command line or used as a service over XML-RPC and has several different user interfaces.

1.2. History and Goals

BitBake was originally a part of the OpenEmbedded project. It was inspired by the Portage package management system used by the Gentoo Linux distribution. On December 7, 2004, OpenEmbedded project team member Chris Larson split the project into two distinct pieces:

* BitBake, a generic task executor

* OpenEmbedded, a metadata set utilized by BitBake

Today, BitBake is the primary basis of the OpenEmbedded [http://www.openembedded.org/] project, which is being used to build and maintain Linux distributions such as the Angstrom Distribution [http://www.angstrom-distribution.org/], and which is also being used as the build tool for Linux projects such as the Yocto Project [http://www.yoctoproject.org].

Prior to BitBake, no other build tool adequately met the needs of an aspiring embedded Linux distribution. All of the build systems used by traditional desktop Linux distributions lacked important functionality, and none of the ad hoc Buildroot-based systems, prevalent in the embedded space, were scalable or maintainable.

Some important original goals for BitBake were:

* Handle cross-compilation.

* Handle inter-package dependencies (build time on target architecture, build time on native architecture, and runtime).

* Support running any number of tasks within a given package, including, but not limited to, fetching upstream sources, unpacking them, patching them, configuring them, and so forth.

* Be Linux distribution agnostic for both build and target systems.

- Be architecture agnostic.

- Support multiple build and target operating systems (e.g. Cygwin, the BSDs, and so forth).

- Be self contained, rather than tightly integrated into the build machine's root filesystem.

- Handle conditional metadata on the target architecture, operating system, distribution, and machine.

- Be easy to use the tools to supply local metadata and packages against which to operate.

- Be easy to use BitBake to collaborate between multiple projects for their builds.

- Provide an inheritance mechanism to share common metadata between many packages.

Over time it became apparent that some further requirements were necessary:

- Handle variants of a base recipe (e.g. native, sdk, and multilib).

- Split metadata into layers and allow layers to enhance or override other layers.

- Allow representation of a given set of input variables to a task as a checksum. Based on that checksum, allow acceleration of builds with prebuilt components.

BitBake satisfies all the original requirements and many more with extensions being made to the basic functionality to reflect the additional requirements. Flexibility and power have always been the priorities. BitBake is highly extensible and supports embedded Python code and execution of any arbitrary tasks.

1.3. Concepts

BitBake is a program written in the Python language. At the highest level, BitBake interprets metadata, decides what tasks are required to run, and executes those tasks. Similar to GNU Make, BitBake controls how software is built. GNU Make achieves its control through "makefiles", while BitBake uses "recipes".

BitBake extends the capabilities of a simple tool like GNU Make by allowing for the definition of much more complex tasks, such as assembling entire embedded Linux distributions.

The remainder of this section introduces several concepts that should be understood in order to better leverage the power of BitBake.

1.3.1. Recipes

BitBake Recipes, which are denoted by the file extension .bb, are the most basic metadata files. These recipe files provide BitBake with the following:

- Descriptive information about the package (author, homepage, license, and so on)

- The version of the recipe

- Existing dependencies (both build and runtime dependencies)

- Where the source code resides and how to fetch it

- Whether the source code requires any patches, where to find them, and how to apply them

- How to configure and compile the source code

- Where on the target machine to install the package or packages created

Within the context of BitBake, or any project utilizing BitBake as its build system, files with the .bb extension are referred to as recipes.

Note
The term "package" is also commonly used to describe recipes. However, since the same word is used to describe packaged output from a project, it is best to maintain a single descriptive

term - "recipes". Put another way, a single "recipe" file is quite capable of generating a number of related but separately installable "packages". In fact, that ability is fairly common.

1.3.2. Configuration Files

Configuration files, which are denoted by the .conf extension, define various configuration variables that govern the project's build process. These files fall into several areas that define machine configuration options, distribution configuration options, compiler tuning options, general common configuration options, and user configuration options. The main configuration file is the sample bitbake.conf file, which is located within the BitBake source tree conf directory.

1.3.3. Classes

Class files, which are denoted by the .bbclass extension, contain information that is useful to share between metadata files. The BitBake source tree currently comes with one class metadata file called base.bbclass. You can find this file in the classes directory. The base.bbclass class files is special since it is always included automatically for all recipes and classes. This class contains definitions for standard basic tasks such as fetching, unpacking, configuring (empty by default), compiling (runs any Makefile present), installing (empty by default) and packaging (empty by default). These tasks are often overridden or extended by other classes added during the project development process.

1.3.4. Layers

Layers allow you to isolate different types of customizations from each other. While you might find it tempting to keep everything in one layer when working on a single project, the more modular you organize your metadata, the easier it is to cope with future changes.

To illustrate how you can use layers to keep things modular, consider customizations you might make to support a specific target machine. These types of customizations typically reside in a special layer, rather than a general layer, called a Board Support Package (BSP) Layer. Furthermore, the machine customizations should be isolated from recipes and metadata that support a new GUI environment, for example. This situation gives you a couple of layers: one for the machine configurations and one for the GUI environment. It is important to understand, however, that the BSP layer can still make machine-specific additions to recipes within the GUI environment layer without polluting the GUI layer itself with those machine-specific changes. You can accomplish this through a recipe that is a BitBake append (.bbappend) file.

1.3.5. Append Files

Append files, which are files that have the .bbappend file extension, extend or override information in an existing recipe file.

BitBake expects every append file to have a corresponding recipe file. Furthermore, the append file and corresponding recipe file must use the same root filename. The filenames can differ only in the file type suffix used (e.g. formfactor_0.0.bb and formfactor_0.0.bbappend).

Information in append files extends or overrides the information in the underlying, similarly-named recipe files.

When you name an append file, you can use the wildcard character (%) to allow for matching recipe names. For example, suppose you have an append file named as follows:

```
busybox_1.21.%.bbappend
```

That append file would match any busybox_1.21.x.bb version of the recipe. So, the append file would match the following recipe names:

```
busybox_1.21.1.bb
busybox_1.21.2.bb
busybox_1.21.3.bb
```

If the busybox recipe was updated to busybox_1.3.0.bb, the append name would not match. However, if you named the append file busybox_1.%.bbappend, then you would have a match.

In the most general case, you could name the append file something as simple as busybox_%.bbappend to be entirely version independent.

1.4. Obtaining BitBake

You can obtain BitBake several different ways:

- Cloning BitBake: Using Git to clone the BitBake source code repository is the recommended method for obtaining BitBake. Cloning the repository makes it easy to get bug fixes and have access to stable branches and the master branch. Once you have cloned BitBake, you should use the latest stable branch for development since the master branch is for BitBake development and might contain less stable changes.

  You usually need a version of BitBake that matches the metadata you are using. The metadata is generally backwards compatible but not forward compatible.

  Here is an example that clones the BitBake repository:

  ```
  $ git clone git://git.openembedded.org/bitbake
  ```

  This command clones the BitBake Git repository into a directory called bitbake. Alternatively, you can designate a directory after the git clone command if you want to call the new directory something other than bitbake. Here is an example that names the directory bbdev:

  ```
  $ git clone git://git.openembedded.org/bitbake bbdev
  ```

- Installation using your Distribution Package Management System: This method is not recommended because the BitBake version that is provided by your distribution, in most cases, is several releases behind a snapshot of the BitBake repository.

- Taking a snapshot of BitBake: Downloading a snapshot of BitBake from the source code repository gives you access to a known branch or release of BitBake.

  ## Note
  Cloning the Git repository, as described earlier, is the preferred method for getting BitBake. Cloning the repository makes it easier to update as patches are added to the stable branches.

  The following example downloads a snapshot of BitBake version 1.17.0:

  ```
  $ wget http://git.openembedded.org/bitbake/snapshot/bitbake-1.17.0.tar.gz
  $ tar zxpvf bitbake-1.17.0.tar.gz
  ```

  After extraction of the tarball using the tar utility, you have a directory entitled bitbake-1.17.0.

- Using the BitBake that Comes With Your Build Checkout: A final possibility for getting a copy of BitBake is that it already comes with your checkout of a larger Bitbake-based build system, such as Poky. Rather than manually checking out individual layers and gluing them together yourself, you can check out an entire build system. The checkout will already include a version of BitBake that has been thoroughly tested for compatibility with the other components. For information on how to check out a particular BitBake-based build system, consult that build system's supporting documentation.

1.5. The BitBake Command

The bitbake command is the primary interface to the BitBake tool. This section presents the BitBake command syntax and provides several execution examples.

1.5.1. Usage and syntax

Following is the usage and syntax for BitBake:

```
$ bitbake -h
Usage: bitbake [options] [recipename/target recipe:do_task ...]

    Executes the specified task (default is 'build') for a given set of target recipes (
    It is assumed there is a conf/bblayers.conf available in cwd or in BBPATH which
    will provide the layer, BBFILES and other configuration information.

Options:
  --version             show program's version number and exit
  -h, --help            show this help message and exit
  -b BUILDFILE, --buildfile=BUILDFILE
                        Execute tasks from a specific .bb recipe directly.
                        WARNING: Does not handle any dependencies from other
                        recipes.
  -k, --continue        Continue as much as possible after an error. While the
                        target that failed and anything depending on it cannot
                        be built, as much as possible will be built before
                        stopping.
  -a, --tryaltconfigs   Continue with builds by trying to use alternative
                        providers where possible.
  -f, --force           Force the specified targets/task to run (invalidating
                        any existing stamp file).
  -c CMD, --cmd=CMD     Specify the task to execute. The exact options
                        available depend on the metadata. Some examples might
                        be 'compile' or 'populate_sysroot' or 'listtasks' may
                        give a list of the tasks available.
  -C INVALIDATE_STAMP, --clear-stamp=INVALIDATE_STAMP
                        Invalidate the stamp for the specified task such as
                        'compile' and then run the default task for the
                        specified target(s).
  -r PREFILE, --read=PREFILE
                        Read the specified file before bitbake.conf.
  -R POSTFILE, --postread=POSTFILE
                        Read the specified file after bitbake.conf.
  -v, --verbose         Enable tracing of shell tasks (with 'set -x').
                        Also print bb.note(...) messages to stdout (in
                        addition to writing them to ${T}/log.do_<task>).
  -D, --debug           Increase the debug level. You can specify this
                        more than once. -D sets the debug level to 1,
                        where only bb.debug(1, ...) messages are printed
                        to stdout; -DD sets the debug level to 2, where
                        both bb.debug(1, ...) and bb.debug(2, ...)
                        messages are printed; etc. Without -D, no debug
                        messages are printed. Note that -D only affects
                        output to stdout. All debug messages are written
                        to ${T}/log.do_taskname, regardless of the debug
                        level.
  -n, --dry-run         Don't execute, just go through the motions.
  -S SIGNATURE_HANDLER, --dump-signatures=SIGNATURE_HANDLER
                        Dump out the signature construction information, with
                        no task execution. The SIGNATURE_HANDLER parameter is
                        passed to the handler. Two common values are none and
                        printdiff but the handler may define more/less. none
                        means only dump the signature, printdiff means compare
                        the dumped signature with the cached one.
  -p, --parse-only      Quit after parsing the BB recipes.
  -s, --show-versions   Show current and preferred versions of all recipes.
  -e, --environment     Show the global or per-recipe environment complete
                        with information about where variables were
```

```
                              set/changed.
    -g, --graphviz            Save dependency tree information for the specified
                              targets in the dot syntax.
    -I EXTRA_ASSUME_PROVIDED, --ignore-deps=EXTRA_ASSUME_PROVIDED
                              Assume these dependencies don't exist and are already
                              provided (equivalent to ASSUME_PROVIDED). Useful to
                              make dependency graphs more appealing
    -l DEBUG_DOMAINS, --log-domains=DEBUG_DOMAINS
                              Show debug logging for the specified logging domains
    -P, --profile             Profile the command and save reports.
    -u UI, --ui=UI            The user interface to use (taskexp, knotty or
                              ncurses - default knotty).
    -t SERVERTYPE, --servertype=SERVERTYPE
                              Choose which server type to use (process or xmlrpc -
                              default process).
    --token=XMLRPCTOKEN       Specify the connection token to be used when
                              connecting to a remote server.
    --revisions-changed       Set the exit code depending on whether upstream
                              floating revisions have changed or not.
    --server-only             Run bitbake without a UI, only starting a server
                              (cooker) process.
    -B BIND, --bind=BIND      The name/address for the bitbake server to bind to.
    --no-setscene             Do not run any setscene tasks. sstate will be ignored
                              and everything needed, built.
    --setscene-only           Only run setscene tasks, don't run any real tasks.
    --remote-server=REMOTE_SERVER
                              Connect to the specified server.
    -m, --kill-server         Terminate the remote server.
    --observe-only            Connect to a server as an observing-only client.
    --status-only             Check the status of the remote bitbake server.
    -w WRITEEVENTLOG, --write-log=WRITEEVENTLOG
                              Writes the event log of the build to a bitbake event
                              json file. Use '' (empty string) to assign the name
                              automatically.
```

1.5.2. Examples

This section presents some examples showing how to use BitBake.

1.5.2.1. Executing a Task Against a Single Recipe

Executing tasks for a single recipe file is relatively simple. You specify the file in question, and BitBake parses it and executes the specified task. If you do not specify a task, BitBake executes the default task, which is "build". BitBake obeys inter-task dependencies when doing so.

The following command runs the build task, which is the default task, on the foo_1.0.bb recipe file:

```
$ bitbake -b foo_1.0.bb
```

The following command runs the clean task on the foo.bb recipe file:

```
$ bitbake -b foo.bb -c clean
```

Note
The "-b" option explicitly does not handle recipe dependencies. Other than for debugging purposes, it is instead recommended that you use the syntax presented in the next section.

1.5.2.2. Executing Tasks Against a Set of Recipe Files

There are a number of additional complexities introduced when one wants to manage multiple .bb files. Clearly there needs to be a way to tell BitBake what files are available and, of those, which you want to execute. There also needs to be a way for each recipe to express its dependencies, both for build-time and runtime. There must be a way for you to express recipe preferences when multiple recipes provide the same functionality, or when there are multiple versions of a recipe.

The bitbake command, when not using "--buildfile" or "-b" only accepts a "PROVIDES". You cannot provide anything else. By default, a recipe file generally "PROVIDES" its "packagename" as shown in the following example:

```
$ bitbake foo
```

This next example "PROVIDES" the package name and also uses the "-c" option to tell BitBake to just execute the do_clean task:

```
$ bitbake -c clean foo
```

1.5.2.3. Executing a List of Task and Recipe Combinations

The BitBake command line supports specifying different tasks for individual targets when you specify multiple targets. For example, suppose you had two targets (or recipes) myfirstrecipe and mysecondrecipe and you needed BitBake to run taskA for the first recipe and taskB for the second recipe:

```
$ bitbake myfirstrecipe:do_taskA mysecondrecipe:do_taskB
```

1.5.2.4. Generating Dependency Graphs

BitBake is able to generate dependency graphs using the dot syntax. You can convert these graphs into images using the dot tool from Graphviz [http://www.graphviz.org].

When you generate a dependency graph, BitBake writes three files to the current working directory:

- recipe-depends.dot: Shows dependencies between recipes (i.e. a collapsed version of task-depends.dot).

- task-depends.dot: Shows dependencies between tasks. These dependencies match BitBake's internal task execution list.

- pn-buildlist: Shows a simple list of targets that are to be built.

To stop depending on common depends, use the "-I" depend option and BitBake omits them from the graph. Leaving this information out can produce more readable graphs. This way, you can remove from the graph DEPENDS from inherited classes such as base.bbclass.

Here are two examples that create dependency graphs. The second example omits depends common in OpenEmbedded from the graph:

```
$ bitbake -g foo

$ bitbake -g -I virtual/kernel -I eglibc foo
```

7

Chapter 2. Execution

The primary purpose for running BitBake is to produce some kind of output such as a single installable package, a kernel, a software development kit, or even a full, board-specific bootable Linux image, complete with bootloader, kernel, and root filesystem. Of course, you can execute the bitbake command with options that cause it to execute single tasks, compile single recipe files, capture or clear data, or simply return information about the execution environment.

This chapter describes BitBake's execution process from start to finish when you use it to create an image. The execution process is launched using the following command form:

```
$ bitbake target
```

For information on the BitBake command and its options, see "The BitBake Command" section.

Note

Prior to executing BitBake, you should take advantage of available parallel thread execution on your build host by setting the BB_NUMBER_THREADS variable in your project's local.conf configuration file.

A common method to determine this value for your build host is to run the following:

```
$ grep processor /proc/cpuinfo
```

This command returns the number of processors, which takes into account hyper-threading. Thus, a quad-core build host with hyper-threading most likely shows eight processors, which is the value you would then assign to BB_NUMBER_THREADS.

A possibly simpler solution is that some Linux distributions (e.g. Debian and Ubuntu) provide the ncpus command.

2.1. Parsing the Base Configuration Metadata

The first thing BitBake does is parse base configuration metadata. Base configuration metadata consists of your project's bblayers.conf file to determine what layers BitBake needs to recognize, all necessary layer.conf files (one from each layer), and bitbake.conf. The data itself is of various types:

• Recipes: Details about particular pieces of software.

• Class Data: An abstraction of common build information (e.g. how to build a Linux kernel).

• Configuration Data: Machine-specific settings, policy decisions, and so forth. Configuration data acts as the glue to bind everything together.

The layer.conf files are used to construct key variables such as BBPATH and BBFILES. BBPATH is used to search for configuration and class files under the conf and classes directories, respectively. BBFILES is used to locate both recipe and recipe append files (.bb and .bbappend). If there is no bblayers.conf file, it is assumed the user has set the BBPATH and BBFILES directly in the environment.

Next, the bitbake.conf file is located using the BBPATH variable that was just constructed. The bitbake.conf file may also include other configuration files using the include or require directives.

Prior to parsing configuration files, Bitbake looks at certain variables, including:

• BB_ENV_WHITELIST

• BB_ENV_EXTRAWHITE

• BB_PRESERVE_ENV

- BB_ORIGENV

- BITBAKE_UI

The first four variables in this list relate to how BitBake treats shell environment variables during task execution. By default, BitBake cleans the environment variables and provides tight control over the shell execution environment. However, through the use of these first four variables, you can apply your control regarding the environment variables allowed to be used by BitBake in the shell during execution of tasks. See the "Passing Information Into the Build Task Environment" section and the information about these variables in the variable glossary for more information on how they work and on how to use them.

The base configuration metadata is global and therefore affects all recipes and tasks that are executed.

BitBake first searches the current working directory for an optional conf/bblayers.conf configuration file. This file is expected to contain a BBLAYERS variable that is a space-delimited list of 'layer' directories. Recall that if BitBake cannot find a bblayers.conf file, then it is assumed the user has set the BBPATH and BBFILES variables directly in the environment.

For each directory (layer) in this list, a conf/layer.conf file is located and parsed with the LAYERDIR variable being set to the directory where the layer was found. The idea is these files automatically set up BBPATH and other variables correctly for a given build directory.

BitBake then expects to find the conf/bitbake.conf file somewhere in the user-specified BBPATH. That configuration file generally has include directives to pull in any other metadata such as files specific to the architecture, the machine, the local environment, and so forth.

Only variable definitions and include directives are allowed in BitBake .conf files. Some variables directly influence BitBake's behavior. These variables might have been set from the environment depending on the environment variables previously mentioned or set in the configuration files. The "Variables Glossary" chapter presents a full list of variables.

After parsing configuration files, BitBake uses its rudimentary inheritance mechanism, which is through class files, to inherit some standard classes. BitBake parses a class when the inherit directive responsible for getting that class is encountered.

The base.bbclass file is always included. Other classes that are specified in the configuration using the INHERIT variable are also included. BitBake searches for class files in a classes subdirectory under the paths in BBPATH in the same way as configuration files.

A good way to get an idea of the configuration files and the class files used in your execution environment is to run the following BitBake command:

```
$ bitbake -e > mybb.log
```

Examining the top of the mybb.log shows you the many configuration files and class files used in your execution environment.

Note

You need to be aware of how BitBake parses curly braces. If a recipe uses a closing curly brace within the function and the character has no leading spaces, BitBake produces a parsing error. If you use a pair of curly braces in a shell function, the closing curly brace must not be located at the start of the line without leading spaces.

Here is an example that causes BitBake to produce a parsing error:

```
fakeroot create_shar() {
    cat << "EOF" > ${SDK_DEPLOY}/${TOOLCHAIN_OUTPUTNAME}.sh
usage()
{
  echo "test"
  ###### The following "}" at the start of the line causes a parsing error ######
```

```
     }
     EOF
     }
```

Writing the recipe this way avoids the error:

```
     fakeroot create_shar() {
         cat << "EOF" > ${SDK_DEPLOY}/${TOOLCHAIN_OUTPUTNAME}.sh
     usage()
     {
       echo "test"
       ######The following "}" with a leading space at the start of the line avoids the error
       }
     EOF
     }
```

2.2. Locating and Parsing Recipes

During the configuration phase, BitBake will have set BBFILES. BitBake now uses it to construct a list of recipes to parse, along with any append files (.bbappend) to apply. BBFILES is a space-separated list of available files and supports wildcards. An example would be:

```
     BBFILES = "/path/to/bbfiles/*.bb /path/to/appends/*.bbappend"
```

BitBake parses each recipe and append file located with BBFILES and stores the values of various variables into the datastore.

Note

Append files are applied in the order they are encountered in BBFILES.
For each file, a fresh copy of the base configuration is made, then the recipe is parsed line by line. Any inherit statements cause BitBake to find and then parse class files (.bbclass) using BBPATH as the search path. Finally, BitBake parses in order any append files found in BBFILES.

One common convention is to use the recipe filename to define pieces of metadata. For example, in bitbake.conf the recipe name and version are used to set the variables PN and PV:

```
     PN = "${@bb.parse.BBHandler.vars_from_file(d.getVar('FILE', False),d)[0] or 'defaultpkgname'
     PV = "${@bb.parse.BBHandler.vars_from_file(d.getVar('FILE', False),d)[1] or '1.0'}"
```

In this example, a recipe called "something_1.2.3.bb" would set PN to "something" and PV to "1.2.3".

By the time parsing is complete for a recipe, BitBake has a list of tasks that the recipe defines and a set of data consisting of keys and values as well as dependency information about the tasks.

BitBake does not need all of this information. It only needs a small subset of the information to make decisions about the recipe. Consequently, BitBake caches the values in which it is interested and does not store the rest of the information. Experience has shown it is faster to re-parse the metadata than to try and write it out to the disk and then reload it.

Where possible, subsequent BitBake commands reuse this cache of recipe information. The validity of this cache is determined by first computing a checksum of the base configuration data (see BB_HASHCONFIG_WHITELIST) and then checking if the checksum matches. If that checksum matches what is in the cache and the recipe and class files have not changed, Bitbake is able to use the cache. BitBake then reloads the cached information about the recipe instead of reparsing it from scratch.

Recipe file collections exist to allow the user to have multiple repositories of .bb files that contain the same exact package. For example, one could easily use them to make one's own local copy of an upstream repository, but with custom modifications that one does not want upstream. Here is an example:

```
BBFILES = "/stuff/openembedded/*/*.bb /stuff/openembedded.modified/*/*.bb"
BBFILE_COLLECTIONS = "upstream local"
BBFILE_PATTERN_upstream = "^/stuff/openembedded/"
BBFILE_PATTERN_local = "^/stuff/openembedded.modified/"
BBFILE_PRIORITY_upstream = "5"
BBFILE_PRIORITY_local = "10"
```

Note

The layers mechanism is now the preferred method of collecting code. While the collections code remains, its main use is to set layer priorities and to deal with overlap (conflicts) between layers.

2.3. Providers

Assuming BitBake has been instructed to execute a target and that all the recipe files have been parsed, BitBake starts to figure out how to build the target. BitBake looks through the PROVIDES list for each of the recipes. A PROVIDES list is the list of names by which the recipe can be known. Each recipe's PROVIDES list is created implicitly through the recipe's PN variable and explicitly through the recipe's PROVIDES variable, which is optional.

When a recipe uses PROVIDES, that recipe's functionality can be found under an alternative name or names other than the implicit PN name. As an example, suppose a recipe named keyboard_1.0.bb contained the following:

```
PROVIDES += "fullkeyboard"
```

The PROVIDES list for this recipe becomes "keyboard", which is implicit, and "fullkeyboard", which is explicit. Consequently, the functionality found in keyboard_1.0.bb can be found under two different names.

2.4. Preferences

The PROVIDES list is only part of the solution for figuring out a target's recipes. Because targets might have multiple providers, BitBake needs to prioritize providers by determining provider preferences.

A common example in which a target has multiple providers is "virtual/kernel", which is on the PROVIDES list for each kernel recipe. Each machine often selects the best kernel provider by using a line similar to the following in the machine configuration file:

```
PREFERRED_PROVIDER_virtual/kernel = "linux-yocto"
```

The default PREFERRED_PROVIDER is the provider with the same name as the target. Bitbake iterates through each target it needs to build and resolves them and their dependencies using this process.

Understanding how providers are chosen is made complicated by the fact that multiple versions might exist for a given provider. BitBake defaults to the highest version of a provider. Version comparisons are made using the same method as Debian. You can use the PREFERRED_VERSION variable to specify a particular version. You can influence the order by using the DEFAULT_PREFERENCE variable.

By default, files have a preference of "0". Setting DEFAULT_PREFERENCE to "-1" makes the recipe unlikely to be used unless it is explicitly referenced. Setting DEFAULT_PREFERENCE to "1" makes it likely the recipe is used. PREFERRED_VERSION overrides any DEFAULT_PREFERENCE setting. DEFAULT_PREFERENCE is often used to mark newer and more experimental recipe versions until they have undergone sufficient testing to be considered stable.

When there are multiple "versions" of a given recipe, BitBake defaults to selecting the most recent version, unless otherwise specified. If the recipe in question has a DEFAULT_PREFERENCE set lower than the other recipes (default is 0), then it will not be selected. This allows the person or persons maintaining the repository of recipe files to specify their preference for the default selected version. Additionally, the user can specify their preferred version.

If the first recipe is named a_1.1.bb, then the PN variable will be set to "a", and the PV variable will be set to 1.1.

Thus, if a recipe named a_1.2.bb exists, BitBake will choose 1.2 by default. However, if you define the following variable in a .conf file that BitBake parses, you can change that preference:

```
PREFERRED_VERSION_a = "1.1"
```

Note

It is common for a recipe to provide two versions -- a stable, numbered (and preferred) version, and a version that is automatically checked out from a source code repository that is considered more "bleeding edge" but can be selected only explicitly.

For example, in the OpenEmbedded codebase, there is a standard, versioned recipe file for BusyBox, busybox_1.22.1.bb, but there is also a Git-based version, busybox_git.bb, which explicitly contains the line

```
DEFAULT_PREFERENCE = "-1"
```

to ensure that the numbered, stable version is always preferred unless the developer selects otherwise.

2.5. Dependencies

Each target BitBake builds consists of multiple tasks such as fetch, unpack, patch, configure, and compile. For best performance on multi-core systems, BitBake considers each task as an independent entity with its own set of dependencies.

Dependencies are defined through several variables. You can find information about variables BitBake uses in the Variables Glossary near the end of this manual. At a basic level, it is sufficient to know that BitBake uses the DEPENDS and RDEPENDS variables when calculating dependencies.

For more information on how BitBake handles dependencies, see the "Dependencies" section.

2.6. The Task List

Based on the generated list of providers and the dependency information, BitBake can now calculate exactly what tasks it needs to run and in what order it needs to run them. The "Executing Tasks" section has more information on how BitBake chooses which task to execute next.

The build now starts with BitBake forking off threads up to the limit set in the BB_NUMBER_THREADS variable. BitBake continues to fork threads as long as there are tasks ready to run, those tasks have all their dependencies met, and the thread threshold has not been exceeded.

It is worth noting that you can greatly speed up the build time by properly setting the BB_NUMBER_THREADS variable.

As each task completes, a timestamp is written to the directory specified by the STAMP variable. On subsequent runs, BitBake looks in the build directory within tmp/stamps and does not rerun tasks that are already completed unless a timestamp is found to be invalid. Currently, invalid timestamps are only considered on a per recipe file basis. So, for example, if the configure stamp has a timestamp greater than the compile timestamp for a given target, then the compile task would rerun. Running the compile task again, however, has no effect on other providers that depend on that target.

The exact format of the stamps is partly configurable. In modern versions of BitBake, a hash is appended to the stamp so that if the configuration changes, the stamp becomes invalid and the task is automatically rerun. This hash, or signature used, is governed by the signature policy that is configured (see the "Checksums (Signatures)" section for information). It is also possible to append extra metadata to the stamp using the [stamp-extra-info] task flag. For example, OpenEmbedded uses this flag to make some tasks machine-specific.

Note

Some tasks are marked as "nostamp" tasks. No timestamp file is created when these tasks are run. Consequently, "nostamp" tasks are always rerun.

For more information on tasks, see the "Tasks" section.

2.7. Executing Tasks

Tasks can be either a shell task or a Python task. For shell tasks, BitBake writes a shell script to ${T}/run.do_taskname.pid and then executes the script. The generated shell script contains all the exported variables, and the shell functions with all variables expanded. Output from the shell script goes to the file ${T}/log.do_taskname.pid. Looking at the expanded shell functions in the run file and the output in the log files is a useful debugging technique.

For Python tasks, BitBake executes the task internally and logs information to the controlling terminal. Future versions of BitBake will write the functions to files similar to the way shell tasks are handled. Logging will be handled in a way similar to shell tasks as well.

The order in which BitBake runs the tasks is controlled by its task scheduler. It is possible to configure the scheduler and define custom implementations for specific use cases. For more information, see these variables that control the behavior:

• BB_SCHEDULER

• BB_SCHEDULERS

It is possible to have functions run before and after a task's main function. This is done using the [prefuncs] and [postfuncs] flags of the task that lists the functions to run.

2.8. Checksums (Signatures)

A checksum is a unique signature of a task's inputs. The signature of a task can be used to determine if a task needs to be run. Because it is a change in a task's inputs that triggers running the task, BitBake needs to detect all the inputs to a given task. For shell tasks, this turns out to be fairly easy because BitBake generates a "run" shell script for each task and it is possible to create a checksum that gives you a good idea of when the task's data changes.

To complicate the problem, some things should not be included in the checksum. First, there is the actual specific build path of a given task - the working directory. It does not matter if the working directory changes because it should not affect the output for target packages. The simplistic approach for excluding the working directory is to set it to some fixed value and create the checksum for the "run" script. BitBake goes one step better and uses the BB_HASHBASE_WHITELIST variable to define a list of variables that should never be included when generating the signatures.

Another problem results from the "run" scripts containing functions that might or might not get called. The incremental build solution contains code that figures out dependencies between shell functions. This code is used to prune the "run" scripts down to the minimum set, thereby alleviating this problem and making the "run" scripts much more readable as a bonus.

So far we have solutions for shell scripts. What about Python tasks? The same approach applies even though these tasks are more difficult. The process needs to figure out what variables a Python function accesses and what functions it calls. Again, the incremental build solution contains code that first figures out the variable and function dependencies, and then creates a checksum for the data used as the input to the task.

Like the working directory case, situations exist where dependencies should be ignored. For these cases, you can instruct the build process to ignore a dependency by using a line like the following:

```
PACKAGE_ARCHS[vardepsexclude] = "MACHINE"
```

This example ensures that the PACKAGE_ARCHS variable does not depend on the value of MACHINE, even if it does reference it.

Equally, there are cases where we need to add dependencies BitBake is not able to find. You can accomplish this by using a line like the following:

```
PACKAGE_ARCHS[vardeps] = "MACHINE"
```

This example explicitly adds the MACHINE variable as a dependency for PACKAGE_ARCHS.

Consider a case with in-line Python, for example, where BitBake is not able to figure out dependencies. When running in debug mode (i.e. using -DDD), BitBake produces output when it discovers something for which it cannot figure out dependencies.

Thus far, this section has limited discussion to the direct inputs into a task. Information based on direct inputs is referred to as the "basehash" in the code. However, there is still the question of a task's indirect inputs - the things that were already built and present in the build directory. The checksum (or signature) for a particular task needs to add the hashes of all the tasks on which the particular task depends. Choosing which dependencies to add is a policy decision. However, the effect is to generate a master checksum that combines the basehash and the hashes of the task's dependencies.

At the code level, there are a variety of ways both the basehash and the dependent task hashes can be influenced. Within the BitBake configuration file, we can give BitBake some extra information to help it construct the basehash. The following statement effectively results in a list of global variable dependency excludes - variables never included in any checksum. This example uses variables from OpenEmbedded to help illustrate the concept:

```
BB_HASHBASE_WHITELIST ?= "TMPDIR FILE PATH PWD BB_TASKHASH BBPATH DL_DIR \
    SSTATE_DIR THISDIR FILESEXTRAPATHS FILE_DIRNAME HOME LOGNAME SHELL TERM \
    USER FILESPATH STAGING_DIR_HOST STAGING_DIR_TARGET COREBASE PRSERV_HOST \
    PRSERV_DUMPDIR PRSERV_DUMPFILE PRSERV_LOCKDOWN PARALLEL_MAKE \
    CCACHE_DIR EXTERNAL_TOOLCHAIN CCACHE CCACHE_DISABLE LICENSE_PATH SDKPKGSUFFIX"
```

The previous example excludes the work directory, which is part of TMPDIR.

The rules for deciding which hashes of dependent tasks to include through dependency chains are more complex and are generally accomplished with a Python function. The code in meta/lib/oe/sstatesig.py shows two examples of this and also illustrates how you can insert your own policy into the system if so desired. This file defines the two basic signature generators OpenEmbedded Core uses: "OEBasic" and "OEBasicHash". By default, there is a dummy "noop" signature handler enabled in BitBake. This means that behavior is unchanged from previous versions. OE-Core uses the "OEBasicHash" signature handler by default through this setting in the bitbake.conf file:

```
BB_SIGNATURE_HANDLER ?= "OEBasicHash"
```

The "OEBasicHash" BB_SIGNATURE_HANDLER is the same as the "OEBasic" version but adds the task hash to the stamp files. This results in any metadata change that changes the task hash, automatically causing the task to be run again. This removes the need to bump PR values, and changes to metadata automatically ripple across the build.

It is also worth noting that the end result of these signature generators is to make some dependency and hash information available to the build. This information includes:

• BB_BASEHASH_task-taskname: The base hashes for each task in the recipe.

• BB_BASEHASH_filename:taskname: The base hashes for each dependent task.

• BBHASHDEPS_filename:taskname: The task dependencies for each task.

• BB_TASKHASH: The hash of the currently running task.

It is worth noting that BitBake's "-S" option lets you debug Bitbake's processing of signatures. The options passed to -S allow different debugging modes to be used, either using BitBake's own debug functions or possibly those defined in the metadata/signature handler itself. The simplest parameter to pass is "none", which causes a set of signature information to be written out into STAMPS_DIR corresponding to the targets specified. The other currently available parameter is "printdiff", which causes BitBake to try to establish the closest signature match it can (e.g. in the sstate cache) and then run bitbake-diffsigs over the matches to determine the stamps and delta where these two stamp trees diverge.

Note
It is likely that future versions of BitBake will provide other signature handlers triggered through additional "-S" parameters.

You can find more information on checksum metadata in the "Task Checksums and Setscene" section.

2.9. Setscene

The setscene process enables BitBake to handle "pre-built" artifacts. The ability to handle and reuse these artifacts allows BitBake the luxury of not having to build something from scratch every time. Instead, BitBake can use, when possible, existing build artifacts.

BitBake needs to have reliable data indicating whether or not an artifact is compatible. Signatures, described in the previous section, provide an ideal way of representing whether an artifact is compatible. If a signature is the same, an object can be reused.

If an object can be reused, the problem then becomes how to replace a given task or set of tasks with the pre-built artifact. BitBake solves the problem with the "setscene" process.

When BitBake is asked to build a given target, before building anything, it first asks whether cached information is available for any of the targets it's building, or any of the intermediate targets. If cached information is available, BitBake uses this information instead of running the main tasks.

BitBake first calls the function defined by the BB_HASHCHECK_FUNCTION variable with a list of tasks and corresponding hashes it wants to build. This function is designed to be fast and returns a list of the tasks for which it believes in can obtain artifacts.

Next, for each of the tasks that were returned as possibilities, BitBake executes a setscene version of the task that the possible artifact covers. Setscene versions of a task have the string "_setscene" appended to the task name. So, for example, the task with the name xxx has a setscene task named xxx_setscene. The setscene version of the task executes and provides the necessary artifacts returning either success or failure.

As previously mentioned, an artifact can cover more than one task. For example, it is pointless to obtain a compiler if you already have the compiled binary. To handle this, BitBake calls the BB_SETSCENE_DEPVALID function for each successful setscene task to know whether or not it needs to obtain the dependencies of that task.

Finally, after all the setscene tasks have executed, BitBake calls the function listed in BB_SETSCENE_VERIFY_FUNCTION2 with the list of tasks BitBake thinks has been "covered". The metadata can then ensure that this list is correct and can inform BitBake that it wants specific tasks to be run regardless of the setscene result.

You can find more information on setscene metadata in the "Task Checksums and Setscene" section.

Chapter 3. Syntax and Operators

Bitbake files have their own syntax. The syntax has similarities to several other languages but also has some unique features. This section describes the available syntax and operators as well as provides examples.

3.1. Basic Syntax

This section provides some basic syntax examples.

3.1.1. Basic Variable Setting

The following example sets VARIABLE to "value". This assignment occurs immediately as the statement is parsed. It is a "hard" assignment.

```
VARIABLE = "value"
```

As expected, if you include leading or trailing spaces as part of an assignment, the spaces are retained:

```
VARIABLE = " value"
VARIABLE = "value "
```

Setting VARIABLE to "" sets it to an empty string, while setting the variable to " " sets it to a blank space (i.e. these are not the same values).

```
VARIABLE = ""
VARIABLE = " "
```

You can use single quotes instead of double quotes when setting a variable's value. Doing so allows you to use values that contain the double quote character:

```
VARIABLE = 'I have a " in my value'
```

Note
Unlike in Bourne shells, single quotes work identically to double quotes in all other ways. They do not suppress variable expansions.

3.1.2. Line Joining

Outside of functions, BitBake joins any line ending in a backslash character ("\") with the following line before parsing statements. The most common use for the "\" character is to split variable assignments over multiple lines, as in the following example:

```
FOO = "bar \
       baz \
       qaz"
```

Both the "\" character and the newline character that follow it are removed when joining lines. Thus, no newline characters end up in the value of FOO.

Consider this additional example where the two assignments both assign "barbaz" to FOO:

```
FOO = "barbaz"

FOO = "bar\
baz"
```

Note

BitBake does not interpret escape sequences like "\n" in variable values. For these to have an effect, the value must be passed to some utility that interprets escape sequences, such as `printf` or `echo -n`.

3.1.3. Variable Expansion

Variables can reference the contents of other variables using a syntax that is similar to variable expansion in Bourne shells. The following assignments result in A containing "aval" and B evaluating to "preavalpost".

```
A = "aval"
B = "pre${A}post"
```

Note

Unlike in Bourne shells, the curly braces are mandatory: Only ${FOO} and not $FOO is recognized as an expansion of FOO.

The "=" operator does not immediately expand variable references in the right-hand side. Instead, expansion is deferred until the variable assigned to is actually used. The result depends on the current values of the referenced variables. The following example should clarify this behavior:

```
A = "${B} baz"
B = "${C} bar"
C = "foo"
*At this point, ${A} equals "foo bar baz"*
C = "qux"
*At this point, ${A} equals "qux bar baz"*
B = "norf"
*At this point, ${A} equals "norf baz"*
```

Contrast this behavior with the immediate variable expansion operator (i.e. ":=").

If the variable expansion syntax is used on a variable that does not exist, the string is kept as is. For example, given the following assignment, BAR expands to the literal string "${FOO}" as long as FOO does not exist.

```
BAR = "${FOO}"
```

3.1.4. Setting a default value (?=)

You can use the "?=" operator to achieve a "softer" assignment for a variable. This type of assignment allows you to define a variable if it is undefined when the statement is parsed, but to leave the value alone if the variable has a value. Here is an example:

```
A ?= "aval"
```

If A is set at the time this statement is parsed, the variable retains its value. However, if A is not set, the variable is set to "aval".

Note

This assignment is immediate. Consequently, if multiple "?=" assignments to a single variable exist, the first of those ends up getting used.

3.1.5. Setting a weak default value (??=)

It is possible to use a "weaker" assignment than in the previous section by using the "??=" operator. This assignment behaves identical to "?=" except that the assignment is made at the end of the parsing process rather than immediately. Consequently, when multiple "??=" assignments exist, the last one is used. Also, any "=" or "?=" assignment will override the value set with "??=". Here is an example:

```
A ??= "somevalue"
A ??= "someothervalue"
```

If A is set before the above statements are parsed, the variable retains its value. If A is not set, the variable is set to "someothervalue".

Again, this assignment is a "lazy" or "weak" assignment because it does not occur until the end of the parsing process.

3.1.6. Immediate variable expansion (:=)

The ":=" operator results in a variable's contents being expanded immediately, rather than when the variable is actually used:

```
T = "123"
A := "${B} ${A} test ${T}"
T = "456"
B = "${T} bval"
C = "cval"
C := "${C}append"
```

In this example, A contains "test 123" because ${B} and ${A} at the time of parsing are undefined, which leaves "test 123". And, the variable C contains "cvalappend" since ${C} immediately expands to "cval".

3.1.7. Appending (+=) and prepending (=+) With Spaces

Appending and prepending values is common and can be accomplished using the "+=" and "=+" operators. These operators insert a space between the current value and prepended or appended value.

These operators take immediate effect during parsing. Here are some examples:

```
B = "bval"
B += "additionaldata"
C = "cval"
C =+ "test"
```

The variable B contains "bval additionaldata" and C contains "test cval".

3.1.8. Appending (.=) and Prepending (=.) Without Spaces

If you want to append or prepend values without an inserted space, use the ".=" and "=." operators.

These operators take immediate effect during parsing. Here are some examples:

```
B = "bval"
B .= "additionaldata"
C = "cval"
C =. "test"
```

The variable B contains "bvaladditionaldata" and C contains "testcval".

3.1.9. Appending and Prepending (Override Style Syntax)

You can also append and prepend a variable's value using an override style syntax. When you use this syntax, no spaces are inserted.

These operators differ from the ":=", ".=", "=.", "+=", and "=+" operators in that their effects are deferred until after parsing completes rather than being immediately applied. Here are some examples:

```
B = "bval"
B_append = " additional data"
C = "cval"
C_prepend = "additional data "
D = "dval"
D_append = "additional data"
```

The variable B becomes "bval additional data" and C becomes "additional data cval". The variable D becomes "dvaladditional data".

Note
You must control all spacing when you use the override syntax.

It is also possible to append and prepend to shell functions and BitBake-style Python functions. See the "Shell Functions" and "BitBake-Style Python Functions sections for examples.

3.1.10. Removal (Override Style Syntax)

You can remove values from lists using the removal override style syntax. Specifying a value for removal causes all occurrences of that value to be removed from the variable.

When you use this syntax, BitBake expects one or more strings. Surrounding spaces are removed as well. Here is an example:

```
FOO = "123 456 789 123456 123 456 123 456"
FOO_remove = "123"
FOO_remove = "456"
FOO2 = "abc def ghi abcdef abc def abc def"
FOO2_remove = "abc def"
```

The variable FOO becomes "789 123456" and FOO2 becomes "ghi abcdef".

Like "_append" and "_prepend", "_remove" is deferred until after parsing completes.

3.1.11. Override Style Operation Advantages

An advantage of the override style operations "_append", "_prepend", and "_remove" as compared to the "+=" and "=+" operators is that the override style operators provide guaranteed operations. For example, consider a class foo.bbclass that needs to add the value "val" to the variable FOO, and a recipe that uses foo.bbclass as follows:

```
inherit foo
```

19

```
FOO = "initial"
```

If foo.bbclass uses the "+=" operator, as follows, then the final value of FOO will be "initial", which is not what is desired:

```
FOO += "val"
```

If, on the other hand, foo.bbclass uses the "_append" operator, then the final value of FOO will be "initial val", as intended:

```
FOO_append = " val"
```

Note
It is never necessary to use "+=" together with "_append". The following sequence of assignments appends "barbaz" to FOO:

```
FOO_append = "bar"
FOO_append = "baz"
```

The only effect of changing the second assignment in the previous example to use "+=" would be to add a space before "baz" in the appended value (due to how the "+=" operator works). Another advantage of the override style operations is that you can combine them with other overrides as described in the "Conditional Syntax (Overrides)" section.

3.1.12. Variable Flag Syntax

Variable flags are BitBake's implementation of variable properties or attributes. It is a way of tagging extra information onto a variable. You can find more out about variable flags in general in the "Variable Flags" section.

You can define, append, and prepend values to variable flags. All the standard syntax operations previously mentioned work for variable flags except for override style syntax (i.e. "_prepend", "_append", and "_remove").

Here are some examples showing how to set variable flags:

```
FOO[a] = "abc"
FOO[b] = "123"
FOO[a] += "456"
```

The variable FOO has two flags: [a] and [b]. The flags are immediately set to "abc" and "123", respectively. The [a] flag becomes "abc 456".

No need exists to pre-define variable flags. You can simply start using them. One extremely common application is to attach some brief documentation to a BitBake variable as follows:

```
CACHE[doc] = "The directory holding the cache of the metadata."
```

3.1.13. Inline Python Variable Expansion

You can use inline Python variable expansion to set variables. Here is an example:

```
DATE = "${@time.strftime('%Y%m%d',time.gmtime())}"
```

20

This example results in the DATE variable being set to the current date.

Probably the most common use of this feature is to extract the value of variables from BitBake's internal data dictionary, d. The following lines select the values of a package name and its version number, respectively:

```
PN = "${@bb.parse.BBHandler.vars_from_file(d.getVar('FILE', False),d)[0] or 'defaultpkgn
PV = "${@bb.parse.BBHandler.vars_from_file(d.getVar('FILE', False),d)[1] or '1.0'}"
```

Note

Inline Python expressions work just like variable expansions insofar as the "=" and ":=" operators are concerned. Given the following assignment, foo() is called each time FOO is expanded:

```
FOO = "${@foo()}"
```

Contrast this with the following immediate assignment, where foo() is only called once, while the assignment is parsed:

```
FOO := "${@foo()}"
```

For a different way to set variables with Python code during parsing, see the "Anonymous Python Functions" section.

3.1.14. Unseting variables

It is possible to completely remove a variable or a variable flag from BitBake's internal data dictionary by using the "unset" keyword. Here is an example:

```
unset DATE
unset do_fetch[noexec]
```

These two statements remove the DATE and the do_fetch[noexec] flag.

3.1.15. Providing Pathnames

When specifying pathnames for use with BitBake, do not use the tilde ("~") character as a shortcut for your home directory. Doing so might cause BitBake to not recognize the path since BitBake does not expand this character in the same way a shell would.

Instead, provide a fuller path as the following example illustrates:

```
BBLAYERS ?= " \
  /home/scott-lenovo/LayerA \
  "
```

3.2. Exporting Variables to the Environment

You can export variables to the environment of running tasks by using the export keyword. For example, in the following example, the do_foo task prints "value from the environment" when run:

```
export ENV_VARIABLE
ENV_VARIABLE = "value from the environment"
```

21

```
do_foo() {
    bbplain "$ENV_VARIABLE"
}
```

Note

BitBake does not expand $ENV_VARIABLE in this case because it lacks the obligatory {}.
Rather, $ENV_VARIABLE is expanded by the shell.

It does not matter whether export ENV_VARIABLE appears before or after assignments to ENV_VARIABLE.

It is also possible to combine export with setting a value for the variable. Here is an example:

```
export ENV_VARIABLE = "variable-value"
```

In the output of bitbake -e, variables that are exported to the environment are preceded by "export".

Among the variables commonly exported to the environment are CC and CFLAGS, which are picked up by many build systems.

3.3. Conditional Syntax (Overrides)

BitBake uses OVERRIDES to control what variables are overridden after BitBake parses recipes and configuration files. This section describes how you can use OVERRIDES as conditional metadata, talks about key expansion in relationship to OVERRIDES, and provides some examples to help with understanding.

3.3.1. Conditional Metadata

You can use OVERRIDES to conditionally select a specific version of a variable and to conditionally append or prepend the value of a variable.

Note

Overrides can only use lower-case characters. Additionally, underscores are not permitted in override names as they are used to separate overrides from each other and from the variable name.

- Selecting a Variable: The OVERRIDES variable is a colon-character-separated list that contains items for which you want to satisfy conditions. Thus, if you have a variable that is conditional on "arm", and "arm" is in OVERRIDES, then the "arm"-specific version of the variable is used rather than the non-conditional version. Here is an example:

```
OVERRIDES = "architecture:os:machine"
TEST = "default"
TEST_os = "osspecific"
TEST_nooverride = "othercondvalue"
```

In this example, the OVERRIDES variable lists three overrides: "architecture", "os", and "machine". The variable TEST by itself has a default value of "default". You select the os-specific version of the TEST variable by appending the "os" override to the variable (i.e.TEST_os).

To better understand this, consider a practical example that assumes an OpenEmbedded metadata-based Linux kernel recipe file. The following lines from the recipe file first set the kernel branch variable KBRANCH to a default value, then conditionally override that value based on the architecture of the build:

```
KBRANCH = "standard/base"
KBRANCH_qemuarm  = "standard/arm-versatile-926ejs"
KBRANCH_qemumips = "standard/mti-malta32"
KBRANCH_qemuppc  = "standard/qemuppc"
```

```
KBRANCH_qemux86   = "standard/common-pc/base"
KBRANCH_qemux86-64 = "standard/common-pc-64/base"
KBRANCH_qemumips64 = "standard/mti-malta64"
```

- Appending and Prepending: BitBake also supports append and prepend operations to variable values based on whether a specific item is listed in OVERRIDES. Here is an example:

```
DEPENDS = "glibc ncurses"
OVERRIDES = "machine:local"
DEPENDS_append_machine = " libmad"
```

In this example, DEPENDS becomes "glibc ncurses libmad".

Again, using an OpenEmbedded metadata-based kernel recipe file as an example, the following lines will conditionally append to the KERNEL_FEATURES variable based on the architecture:

```
KERNEL_FEATURES_append = " ${KERNEL_EXTRA_FEATURES}"
KERNEL_FEATURES_append_qemux86=" cfg/sound.scc cfg/paravirt_kvm.scc"
KERNEL_FEATURES_append_qemux86-64=" cfg/sound.scc cfg/paravirt_kvm.scc"
```

- Setting a Variable for a Single Task: BitBake supports setting a variable just for the duration of a single task. Here is an example:

```
FOO_task-configure = "val 1"
FOO_task-compile = "val 2"
```

In the previous example, FOO has the value "val 1" while the do_configure task is executed, and the value "val 2" while the do_compile task is executed.

Internally, this is implemented by prepending the task (e.g. "task-compile:") to the value of OVERRIDES for the local datastore of the do_compile task.

You can also use this syntax with other combinations (e.g. "_prepend") as shown in the following example:

```
EXTRA_OEMAKE_prepend_task-compile = "${PARALLEL_MAKE} "
```

3.3.2. Key Expansion

Key expansion happens when the BitBake datastore is finalized just before BitBake expands overrides. To better understand this, consider the following example:

```
A${B} = "X"
B = "2"
A2 = "Y"
```

In this case, after all the parsing is complete, and before any overrides are handled, BitBake expands ${B} into "2". This expansion causes A2, which was set to "Y" before the expansion, to become "X".

3.3.3. Examples

Despite the previous explanations that show the different forms of variable definitions, it can be hard to work out exactly what happens when variable operators, conditional overrides, and unconditional overrides are combined. This section presents some common scenarios along with explanations for variable interactions that typically confuse users.

There is often confusion concerning the order in which overrides and various "append" operators take effect. Recall that an append or prepend operation using "_append" and "_prepend" does not result in an immediate assignment as would "+=", ".=", "=+", or "=.". Consider the following example:

```
OVERRIDES = "foo"
A = "Z"
A_foo_append = "X"
```

For this case, A is unconditionally set to "Z" and "X" is unconditionally and immediately appended to the variable A_foo. Because overrides have not been applied yet, A_foo is set to "X" due to the append and A simply equals "Z".

Applying overrides, however, changes things. Since "foo" is listed in OVERRIDES, the conditional variable A is replaced with the "foo" version, which is equal to "X". So effectively, A_foo replaces A.

This next example changes the order of the override and the append:

```
OVERRIDES = "foo"
A = "Z"
A_append_foo = "X"
```

For this case, before overrides are handled, A is set to "Z" and A_append_foo is set to "X". Once the override for "foo" is applied, however, A gets appended with "X". Consequently, A becomes "ZX". Notice that spaces are not appended.

This next example has the order of the appends and overrides reversed back as in the first example:

```
OVERRIDES = "foo"
A = "Y"
A_foo_append = "Z"
A_foo_append = "X"
```

For this case, before any overrides are resolved, A is set to "Y" using an immediate assignment. After this immediate assignment, A_foo is set to "Z", and then further appended with "X" leaving the variable set to "ZX". Finally, applying the override for "foo" results in the conditional variable A becoming "ZX" (i.e. A is replaced with A_foo).

This final example mixes in some varying operators:

```
A = "1"
A_append = "2"
A_append = "3"
A += "4"
A .= "5"
```

For this case, the type of append operators are affecting the order of assignments as BitBake passes through the code multiple times. Initially, A is set to "1 45" because of the three statements that use immediate operators. After these assignments are made, BitBake applies the "_append" operations. Those operations result in A becoming "1 4523".

3.4. Sharing Functionality

BitBake allows for metadata sharing through include files (.inc) and class files (.bbclass). For example, suppose you have a piece of common functionality such as a task definition that you want to share between more than one recipe. In this case, creating a .bbclass file that contains the common functionality and then using the inherit directive in your recipes to inherit the class would be a common way to share the task.

This section presents the mechanisms BitBake provides to allow you to share functionality between recipes. Specifically, the mechanisms include include, inherit, INHERIT, and require directives.

3.4.1. Locating Include and Class Files

BitBake uses the BBPATH variable to locate needed include and class files. Additionally, BitBake searches the current directory for include and require directives.

Note

The BBPATH variable is analogous to the environment variable PATH.

In order for include and class files to be found by BitBake, they need to be located in a "classes" subdirectory that can be found in BBPATH.

3.4.2. inherit Directive

When writing a recipe or class file, you can use the inherit directive to inherit the functionality of a class (.bbclass). BitBake only supports this directive when used within recipe and class files (i.e. .bb and .bbclass).

The inherit directive is a rudimentary means of specifying functionality contained in class files that your recipes require. For example, you can easily abstract out the tasks involved in building a package that uses Autoconf and Automake and put those tasks into a class file and then have your recipe inherit that class file.

As an example, your recipes could use the following directive to inherit an autotools.bbclass file. The class file would contain common functionality for using Autotools that could be shared across recipes:

```
inherit autotools
```

In this case, BitBake would search for the directory classes/autotools.bbclass in BBPATH.

Note

You can override any values and functions of the inherited class within your recipe by doing so after the "inherit" statement.

If you want to use the directive to inherit multiple classes, separate them with spaces. The following example shows how to inherit both the buildhistory and rm_work classes:

```
inherit buildhistory rm_work
```

An advantage with the inherit directive as compared to both the include and require directives is that you can inherit class files conditionally. You can accomplish this by using a variable expression after the inherit statement. Here is an example:

```
inherit ${VARNAME}
```

If VARNAME is going to be set, it needs to be set before the inherit statement is parsed. One way to achieve a conditional inherit in this case is to use overrides:

```
VARIABLE = ""
VARIABLE_someoverride = "myclass"
```

Another method is by using anonymous Python. Here is an example:

```
python () {
    if condition == value:
        d.setVar('VARIABLE', 'myclass')
```

```
        else:
            d.setVar('VARIABLE', '')
    }
```

Alternatively, you could use an in-line Python expression in the following form:

```
    inherit ${@'classname' if condition else ''}
    inherit ${@functionname(params)}
```

In all cases, if the expression evaluates to an empty string, the statement does not trigger a syntax error because it becomes a no-op.

3.4.3. `include` Directive

BitBake understands the `include` directive. This directive causes BitBake to parse whatever file you specify, and to insert that file at that location. The directive is much like its equivalent in Make except that if the path specified on the include line is a relative path, BitBake locates the first file it can find within BBPATH.

The include directive is a more generic method of including functionality as compared to the inherit directive, which is restricted to class (i.e. `.bbclass`) files. The include directive is applicable for any other kind of shared or encapsulated functionality or configuration that does not suit a `.bbclass` file.

As an example, suppose you needed a recipe to include some self-test definitions:

```
    include test_defs.inc
```

Note

The `include` directive does not produce an error when the file cannot be found. Consequently, it is recommended that if the file you are including is expected to exist, you should use `require` instead of `include`. Doing so makes sure that an error is produced if the file cannot be found.

3.4.4. `require` Directive

BitBake understands the `require` directive. This directive behaves just like the `include` directive with the exception that BitBake raises a parsing error if the file to be included cannot be found. Thus, any file you require is inserted into the file that is being parsed at the location of the directive.

The require directive, like the include directive previously described, is a more generic method of including functionality as compared to the inherit directive, which is restricted to class (i.e. `.bbclass`) files. The require directive is applicable for any other kind of shared or encapsulated functionality or configuration that does not suit a `.bbclass` file.

Similar to how BitBake handles include, if the path specified on the require line is a relative path, BitBake locates the first file it can find within BBPATH.

As an example, suppose you have two versions of a recipe (e.g. `foo_1.2.2.bb` and `foo_2.0.0.bb`) where each version contains some identical functionality that could be shared. You could create an include file named `foo.inc` that contains the common definitions needed to build "foo". You need to be sure `foo.inc` is located in the same directory as your two recipe files as well. Once these conditions are set up, you can share the functionality using a `require` directive from within each recipe:

```
    require foo.inc
```

3.4.5. **INHERIT** Configuration Directive

When creating a configuration file (`.conf`), you can use the INHERIT configuration directive to inherit a class. BitBake only supports this directive when used within a configuration file.

As an example, suppose you needed to inherit a class file called abc.bbclass from a configuration file as follows:

```
INHERIT += "abc"
```

This configuration directive causes the named class to be inherited at the point of the directive during parsing. As with the inherit directive, the .bbclass file must be located in a "classes" subdirectory in one of the directories specified in BBPATH.

Note

Because .conf files are parsed first during BitBake's execution, using INHERIT to inherit a class effectively inherits the class globally (i.e. for all recipes).

If you want to use the directive to inherit multiple classes, you can provide them on the same line in the local.conf file. Use spaces to separate the classes. The following example shows how to inherit both the autotools and pkgconfig classes:

```
INHERIT += "autotools pkgconfig"
```

3.5. Functions

As with most languages, functions are the building blocks that are used to build up operations into tasks. BitBake supports these types of functions:

• Shell Functions: Functions written in shell script and executed either directly as functions, tasks, or both. They can also be called by other shell functions.

• BitBake-Style Python Functions: Functions written in Python and executed by BitBake or other Python functions using bb.build.exec_func().

• Python Functions: Functions written in Python and executed by Python.

• Anonymous Python Functions: Python functions executed automatically during parsing.

Regardless of the type of function, you can only define them in class (.bbclass) and recipe (.bb or .inc) files.

3.5.1. Shell Functions

Functions written in shell script and executed either directly as functions, tasks, or both. They can also be called by other shell functions. Here is an example shell function definition:

```
some_function () {
    echo "Hello World"
}
```

When you create these types of functions in your recipe or class files, you need to follow the shell programming rules. The scripts are executed by /bin/sh, which may not be a bash shell but might be something such as dash. You should not use Bash-specific script (bashisms).

Overrides and override-style operators like _append and _prepend can also be applied to shell functions. Most commonly, this application would be used in a .bbappend file to modify functions in the main recipe. It can also be used to modify functions inherited from classes.

As an example, consider the following:

```
do_foo() {
    bbplain first
    fn
```

```
    }

    fn_prepend() {
        bbplain second
    }

    fn() {
        bbplain third
    }

    do_foo_append() {
        bbplain fourth
    }
```

Running do_foo prints the following:

```
    recipename do_foo: first
    recipename do_foo: second
    recipename do_foo: third
    recipename do_foo: fourth
```

Note

Overrides and override-style operators can be applied to any shell function, not just tasks.
You can use the bitbake -e recipename command to view the final assembled function after all overrides have been applied.

3.5.2. BitBake-Style Python Functions

These functions are written in Python and executed by BitBake or other Python functions using bb.build.exec_func().

An example BitBake function is:

```
    python some_python_function () {
        d.setVar("TEXT", "Hello World")
        print d.getVar("TEXT")
    }
```

Because the Python "bb" and "os" modules are already imported, you do not need to import these modules. Also in these types of functions, the datastore ("d") is a global variable and is always automatically available.

Note

Variable expressions (e.g. ${X}) are no longer expanded within Python functions. This behavior is intentional in order to allow you to freely set variable values to expandable expressions without having them expanded prematurely. If you do wish to expand a variable within a Python function, use d.getVar("X"). Or, for more complicated expressions, use d.expand().

Similar to shell functions, you can also apply overrides and override-style operators to BitBake-style Python functions.

As an example, consider the following:

```
    python do_foo_prepend() {
        bb.plain("first")
    }

    python do_foo() {
```

```
        bb.plain("second")
    }

    python do_foo_append() {
        bb.plain("third")
    }
```

Running do_foo prints the following:

```
    recipename do_foo: first
    recipename do_foo: second
    recipename do_foo: third
```

You can use the bitbake -e recipename command to view the final assembled function after all overrides have been applied.

3.5.3. Python Functions

These functions are written in Python and are executed by other Python code. Examples of Python functions are utility functions that you intend to call from in-line Python or from within other Python functions. Here is an example:

```
    def get_depends(d):
        if d.getVar('SOMECONDITION'):
            return "dependencywithcond"
        else:
            return "dependency"
    SOMECONDITION = "1"
    DEPENDS = "${@get_depends(d)}"
```

This would result in DEPENDS containing dependencywithcond.

Here are some things to know about Python functions:

• Python functions can take parameters.

• The BitBake datastore is not automatically available. Consequently, you must pass it in as a parameter to the function.

• The "bb" and "os" Python modules are automatically available. You do not need to import them.

3.5.4. Bitbake-Style Python Functions Versus Python Functions

Following are some important differences between BitBake-style Python functions and regular Python functions defined with "def":

• Only BitBake-style Python functions can be tasks.

• Overrides and override-style operators can only be applied to BitBake-style Python functions.

• Only regular Python functions can take arguments and return values.

• Variable flags such as [dirs], [cleandirs], and [lockfiles] can be used on BitBake-style Python functions, but not on regular Python functions.

• BitBake-style Python functions generate a separate ${T}/run.function-name.pid script that is executed to run the function, and also generate a log file in ${T}/log.function-name.pid if they are executed as tasks.

Regular Python functions execute "inline" and do not generate any files in ${T}.

29

- Regular Python functions are called with the usual Python syntax. BitBake-style Python functions are usually tasks and are called directly by BitBake, but can also be called manually from Python code by using the bb.build.exec_func() function. Here is an example:

```
bb.build.exec_func("my_bitbake_style_function", d)
```

Note

bb.build.exec_func() can also be used to run shell functions from Python code. If you want to run a shell function before a Python function within the same task, then you can use a parent helper Python function that starts by running the shell function with bb.build.exec_func() and then runs the Python code.

To detect errors from functions executed with bb.build.exec_func(), you can catch the bb.build.FuncFailed exception.

Note

Functions in metadata (recipes and classes) should not themselves raise bb.build.FuncFailed. Rather, bb.build.FuncFailed should be viewed as a general indicator that the called function failed by raising an exception. For example, an exception raised by bb.fatal() will be caught inside bb.build.exec_func(), and a bb.build.FuncFailed will be raised in response.

Due to their simplicity, you should prefer regular Python functions over BitBake-style Python functions unless you need a feature specific to BitBake-style Python functions. Regular Python functions in metadata are a more recent invention than BitBake-style Python functions, and older code tends to use bb.build.exec_func() more often.

3.5.5. Anonymous Python Functions

Sometimes it is useful to set variables or perform other operations programmatically during parsing. To do this, you can define special Python functions, called anonymous Python functions, that run at the end of parsing. For example, the following conditionally sets a variable based on the value of another variable:

```
python () {
    if d.getVar('SOMEVAR') == 'value':
        d.setVar('ANOTHERVAR', 'value2')
}
```

An equivalent way to mark a function as an anonymous function is to give it the name "__anonymous", rather than no name.

Anonymous Python functions always run at the end of parsing, regardless of where they are defined. If a recipe contains many anonymous functions, they run in the same order as they are defined within the recipe. As an example, consider the following snippet:

```
python () {
    d.setVar('FOO', 'foo 2')
}

FOO = "foo 1"

python () {
    d.appendVar('BAR', ' bar 2')
}

BAR = "bar 1"
```

The previous example is conceptually equivalent to the following snippet:

```
FOO = "foo 1"
BAR = "bar 1"
FOO = "foo 2"
BAR += "bar 2"
```

FOO ends up with the value "foo 2", and BAR with the value "bar 1 bar 2". Just as in the second snippet, the values set for the variables within the anonymous functions become available to tasks, which always run after parsing.

Overrides and override-style operators such as "_append" are applied before anonymous functions run. In the following example, FOO ends up with the value "foo from anonymous":

```
FOO = "foo"
FOO_append = " from outside"

python () {
    d.setVar("FOO", "foo from anonymous")
}
```

For methods you can use with anonymous Python functions, see the "Functions You Can Call From Within Python" section. For a different method to run Python code during parsing, see the "Inline Python Variable Expansion" section.

3.5.6. Flexible Inheritance for Class Functions

Through coding techniques and the use of EXPORT_FUNCTIONS, BitBake supports exporting a function from a class such that the class function appears as the default implementation of the function, but can still be called if a recipe inheriting the class needs to define its own version of the function.

To understand the benefits of this feature, consider the basic scenario where a class defines a task function and your recipe inherits the class. In this basic scenario, your recipe inherits the task function as defined in the class. If desired, your recipe can add to the start and end of the function by using the "_prepend" or "_append" operations respectively, or it can redefine the function completely. However, if it redefines the function, there is no means for it to call the class version of the function. EXPORT_FUNCTIONS provides a mechanism that enables the recipe's version of the function to call the original version of the function.

To make use of this technique, you need the following things in place:

• The class needs to define the function as follows:

```
classname_functionname
```

For example, if you have a class file bar.bbclass and a function named do_foo, the class must define the function as follows:

```
bar_do_foo
```

• The class needs to contain the EXPORT_FUNCTIONS statement as follows:

```
EXPORT_FUNCTIONS functionname
```

For example, continuing with the same example, the statement in the bar.bbclass would be as follows:

```
EXPORT_FUNCTIONS do_foo
```

31

- You need to call the function appropriately from within your recipe. Continuing with the same example, if your recipe needs to call the class version of the function, it should call bar_do_foo. Assuming do_foo was a shell function and EXPORT_FUNCTIONS was used as above, the recipe's function could conditionally call the class version of the function as follows:

```
do_foo() {
        if [ somecondition ] ; then
                bar_do_foo
        else
                # Do something else
        fi
}
```

To call your modified version of the function as defined in your recipe, call it as do_foo.

With these conditions met, your single recipe can freely choose between the original function as defined in the class file and the modified function in your recipe. If you do not set up these conditions, you are limited to using one function or the other.

3.6. Tasks

Tasks are BitBake execution units that make up the steps that BitBake can run for a given recipe. Tasks are only supported in recipes and classes (i.e. in .bb files and files included or inherited from .bb files). By convention, tasks have names that start with "do_".

3.6.1. Promoting a Function to a Task

Tasks are either shell functions or BitBake-style Python functions that have been promoted to tasks by using the addtask command. The addtask command can also optionally describe dependencies between the task and other tasks. Here is an example that shows how to define a task and declare some dependencies:

```
python do_printdate () {
    import time
    print time.strftime('%Y%m%d', time.gmtime())
}
addtask printdate after do_fetch before do_build
```

The first argument to addtask is the name of the function to promote to a task. If the name does not start with "do_", "do_" is implicitly added, which enforces the convention that all task names start with "do_".

In the previous example, the do_printdate task becomes a dependency of the do_build task, which is the default task (i.e. the task run by the bitbake command unless another task is specified explicitly). Additionally, the do_printdate task becomes dependent upon the do_fetch task. Running the do_build task results in the do_printdate task running first.

Note

If you try out the previous example, you might see that the do_printdate task is only run the first time you build the recipe with the bitbake command. This is because BitBake considers the task "up-to-date" after that initial run. If you want to force the task to always be rerun for experimentation purposes, you can make BitBake always consider the task "out-of-date" by using the [nostamp] variable flag, as follows:

```
do_printdate[nostamp] = "1"
```

You can also explicitly run the task and provide the -f option as follows:

```
$ bitbake recipe -c printdate -f
```

When manually selecting a task to run with the `bitbake recipe -c task` command, you can omit the "do_" prefix as part of the task name.

You might wonder about the practical effects of using `addtask` without specifying any dependencies as is done in the following example:

```
addtask printdate
```

In this example, assuming dependencies have not been added through some other means, the only way to run the task is by explicitly selecting it with `bitbake recipe -c printdate`. You can use the `do_listtasks` task to list all tasks defined in a recipe as shown in the following example:

```
$ bitbake recipe -c listtasks
```

For more information on task dependencies, see the "Dependencies" section.

See the "Variable Flags" section for information on variable flags you can use with tasks.

3.6.2. Deleting a Task

As well as being able to add tasks, you can delete them. Simply use the `deltask` command to delete a task. For example, to delete the example task used in the previous sections, you would use:

```
deltask printdate
```

If you delete a task using the `deltask` command and the task has dependencies, the dependencies are not reconnected. For example, suppose you have three tasks named do_a, do_b, and do_c. Furthermore, do_c is dependent on do_b, which in turn is dependent on do_a. Given this scenario, if you use `deltask` to delete do_b, the implicit dependency relationship between do_c and do_a through do_b no longer exists, and do_c dependencies are not updated to include do_a. Thus, do_c is free to run before do_a.

If you want dependencies such as these to remain intact, use the [noexec] varflag to disable the task instead of using the `deltask` command to delete it:

```
do_b[noexec] = "1"
```

3.6.3. Passing Information Into the Build Task Environment

When running a task, BitBake tightly controls the shell execution environment of the build tasks to make sure unwanted contamination from the build machine cannot influence the build.

Note
By default, BitBake cleans the environment to include only those things exported or listed in its whitelist to ensure that the build environment is reproducible and consistent. You can prevent this "cleaning" by setting the BB_PRESERVE_ENV variable.

Consequently, if you do want something to get passed into the build task environment, you must take these two steps:

1. Tell BitBake to load what you want from the environment into the datastore. You can do so through the BB_ENV_WHITELIST and BB_ENV_EXTRAWHITE variables. For example, assume you want to

prevent the build system from accessing your $HOME/.ccache directory. The following command "whitelists" the environment variable CCACHE_DIR causing BitBack to allow that variable into the datastore:

```
export BB_ENV_EXTRAWHITE="$BB_ENV_EXTRAWHITE CCACHE_DIR"
```

2. Tell BitBake to export what you have loaded into the datastore to the task environment of every running task. Loading something from the environment into the datastore (previous step) only makes it available in the datastore. To export it to the task environment of every running task, use a command similar to the following in your local configuration file local.conf or your distribution configuration file:

```
export CCACHE_DIR
```

Note

A side effect of the previous steps is that BitBake records the variable as a dependency of the build process in things like the setscene checksums. If doing so results in unnecessary rebuilds of tasks, you can whitelist the variable so that the setscene code ignores the dependency when it creates checksums.

Sometimes, it is useful to be able to obtain information from the original execution environment. Bitbake saves a copy of the original environment into a special variable named BB_ORIGENV.

The BB_ORIGENV variable returns a datastore object that can be queried using the standard datastore operators such as getVar(, False). The datastore object is useful, for example, to find the original DISPLAY variable. Here is an example:

```
origenv = d.getVar("BB_ORIGENV", False)
bar = origenv.getVar("BAR", False)
```

The previous example returns BAR from the original execution environment.

3.7. Variable Flags

Variable flags (varflags) help control a task's functionality and dependencies. BitBake reads and writes varflags to the datastore using the following command forms:

```
variable = d.getVarFlags("variable")
self.d.setVarFlags("FOO", {"func": True})
```

When working with varflags, the same syntax, with the exception of overrides, applies. In other words, you can set, append, and prepend varflags just like variables. See the "Variable Flag Syntax" section for details.

BitBake has a defined set of varflags available for recipes and classes. Tasks support a number of these flags which control various functionality of the task:

- [cleandirs]: Empty directories that should be created before the task runs. Directories that already exist are removed and recreated to empty them.

- [depends]: Controls inter-task dependencies. See the DEPENDS variable and the "Inter-Task Dependencies" section for more information.

- [deptask]: Controls task build-time dependencies. See the DEPENDS variable and the "Build Dependencies" section for more information.

- [dirs]: Directories that should be created before the task runs. Directories that already exist are left as is. The last directory listed is used as the current working directory for the task.

- [lockfiles]: Specifies one or more lockfiles to lock while the task executes. Only one task may hold a lockfile, and any task that attempts to lock an already locked file will block until the lock is released. You can use this variable flag to accomplish mutual exclusion.

- [noexec]: When set to "1", marks the task as being empty, with no execution required. You can use the [noexec] flag to set up tasks as dependency placeholders, or to disable tasks defined elsewhere that are not needed in a particular recipe.

- [nostamp]: When set to "1", tells BitBake to not generate a stamp file for a task, which implies the task should always be executed.

  ### Caution
  Any task that depends (possibly indirectly) on a [nostamp] task will always be executed as well. This can cause unnecessary rebuilding if you are not careful.

- [postfuncs]: List of functions to call after the completion of the task.

- [prefuncs]: List of functions to call before the task executes.

- [rdepends]: Controls inter-task runtime dependencies. See the RDEPENDS variable, the RRECOMMENDS variable, and the "Inter-Task Dependencies" section for more information.

- [rdeptask]: Controls task runtime dependencies. See the RDEPENDS variable, the RRECOMMENDS variable, and the "Runtime Dependencies" section for more information.

- [recideptask]: When set in conjunction with recrdeptask, specifies a task that should be inspected for additional dependencies.

- [recrdeptask]: Controls task recursive runtime dependencies. See the RDEPENDS variable, the RRECOMMENDS variable, and the "Recursive Dependencies" section for more information.

- [stamp-extra-info]: Extra stamp information to append to the task's stamp. As an example, OpenEmbedded uses this flag to allow machine-specific tasks.

- [umask]: The umask to run the task under.

Several varflags are useful for controlling how signatures are calculated for variables. For more information on this process, see the "Checksums (Signatures)" section.

- [vardeps]: Specifies a space-separated list of additional variables to add to a variable's dependencies for the purposes of calculating its signature. Adding variables to this list is useful, for example, when a function refers to a variable in a manner that does not allow BitBake to automatically determine that the variable is referred to.

- [vardepsexclude]: Specifies a space-separated list of variables that should be excluded from a variable's dependencies for the purposes of calculating its signature.

- [vardepvalue]: If set, instructs BitBake to ignore the actual value of the variable and instead use the specified value when calculating the variable's signature.

- [vardepvalueexclude]: Specifies a pipe-separated list of strings to exclude from the variable's value when calculating the variable's signature.

3.8. Events

BitBake allows installation of event handlers within recipe and class files. Events are triggered at certain points during operation, such as the beginning of operation against a given recipe (i.e. *.bb), the start of a given task, a task failure, a task success, and so forth. The intent is to make it easy to do things like email notification on build failures.

Following is an example event handler that prints the name of the event and the content of the FILE variable:

```
addhandler myclass_eventhandler
python myclass_eventhandler() {
```

```
        from bb.event import getName
        print("The name of the Event is %s" % getName(e))
        print("The file we run for is %s" % d.getVar('FILE'))
    }
    myclass_eventhandler[eventmask] = "bb.event.BuildStarted bb.event.BuildCompleted"
```

In the previous example, an eventmask has been set so that the handler only sees the "BuildStarted" and "BuildCompleted" events. This event handler gets called every time an event matching the eventmask is triggered. A global variable "e" is defined, which represents the current event. With the getName(e) method, you can get the name of the triggered event. The global datastore is available as "d". In legacy code, you might see "e.data" used to get the datastore. However, realize that "e.data" is deprecated and you should use "d" going forward.

The context of the datastore is appropriate to the event in question. For example, "BuildStarted" and "BuildCompleted" events run before any tasks are executed so would be in the global configuration datastore namespace. No recipe-specific metadata exists in that namespace. The "BuildStarted" and "BuildCompleted" events also run in the main cooker/server process rather than any worker context. Thus, any changes made to the datastore would be seen by other cooker/server events within the current build but not seen outside of that build or in any worker context. Task events run in the actual tasks in question consequently have recipe-specific and task-specific contents. These events run in the worker context and are discarded at the end of task execution.

During a standard build, the following common events might occur. The following events are the most common kinds of events that most metadata might have an interest in viewing:

- bb.event.ConfigParsed(): Fired when the base configuration; which consists of bitbake.conf, base.bbclass and any global INHERIT statements; has been parsed. You can see multiple such events when each of the workers parse the base configuration or if the server changes configuration and reparses. Any given datastore only has one such event executed against it, however. If BB_INVALIDCONF is set in the datastore by the event handler, the configuration is reparsed and a new event triggered, allowing the metadata to update configuration.

- bb.event.HeartbeatEvent(): Fires at regular time intervals of one second. You can configure the interval time using the BB_HEARTBEAT_EVENT variable. The event's "time" attribute is the time.time() value when the event is triggered. This event is useful for activities such as system state monitoring.

- bb.event.ParseStarted(): Fired when BitBake is about to start parsing recipes. This event's "total" attribute represents the number of recipes BitBake plans to parse.

- bb.event.ParseProgress(): Fired as parsing progresses. This event's "current" attribute is the number of recipes parsed as well as the "total" attribute.

- bb.event.ParseCompleted(): Fired when parsing is complete. This event's "cached", "parsed", "skipped", "virtuals", "masked", and "errors" attributes provide statistics for the parsing results.

- bb.event.BuildStarted(): Fired when a new build starts.

- bb.build.TaskStarted(): Fired when a task starts. This event's "taskfile" attribute points to the recipe from which the task originates. The "taskname" attribute, which is the task's name, includes the do_ prefix, and the "logfile" attribute point to where the task's output is stored. Finally, the "time" attribute is the task's execution start time.

- bb.build.TaskInvalid(): Fired if BitBake tries to execute a task that does not exist.

- bb.build.TaskFailedSilent(): Fired for setscene tasks that fail and should not be presented to the user verbosely.

- bb.build.TaskFailed(): Fired for normal tasks that fail.

- bb.build.TaskSucceeded(): Fired when a task successfully completes.

- bb.event.BuildCompleted(): Fired when a build finishes.

- bb.cooker.CookerExit(): Fired when the BitBake server/cooker shuts down. This event is usually only seen by the UIs as a sign they should also shutdown.

This next list of example events occur based on specific requests to the server. These events are often used to communicate larger pieces of information from the BitBake server to other parts of BitBake such as user interfaces:

- bb.event.TreeDataPreparationStarted()

- bb.event.TreeDataPreparationProgress()

- bb.event.TreeDataPreparationCompleted()

- bb.event.DepTreeGenerated()

- bb.event.CoreBaseFilesFound()

- bb.event.ConfigFilePathFound()

- bb.event.FilesMatchingFound()

- bb.event.ConfigFilesFound()

- bb.event.TargetsTreeGenerated()

3.9. Variants - Class Extension Mechanism

BitBake supports two features that facilitate creating from a single recipe file multiple incarnations of that recipe file where all incarnations are buildable. These features are enabled through the BBCLASSEXTEND and BBVERSIONS variables.

Note
The mechanism for this class extension is extremely specific to the implementation. Usually, the recipe's PROVIDES, PN, and DEPENDS variables would need to be modified by the extension class. For specific examples, see the OE-Core native, nativesdk, and multilib classes.

- BBCLASSEXTEND: This variable is a space separated list of classes used to "extend" the recipe for each variant. Here is an example that results in a second incarnation of the current recipe being available. This second incarnation will have the "native" class inherited.

```
BBCLASSEXTEND = "native"
```

- BBVERSIONS: This variable allows a single recipe to build multiple versions of a project from a single recipe file. You can also specify conditional metadata (using the OVERRIDES mechanism) for a single version, or an optionally named range of versions. Here is an example:

```
BBVERSIONS = "1.0 2.0 git"
SRC_URI_git = "git://someurl/somepath.git"

BBVERSIONS = "1.0.[0-6]:1.0.0+ \ 1.0.[7-9]:1.0.7+"
SRC_URI_append_1.0.7+ = "file://some_patch_which_the_new_versions_need.patch;patch=1"
```

The name of the range defaults to the original version of the recipe. For example, in OpenEmbedded, the recipe file foo_1.0.0+.bb creates a default name range of 1.0.0+. This is useful because the range name is not only placed into overrides, but it is also made available for the metadata to use in the variable that defines the base recipe versions for use in file:// search paths (FILESPATH).

3.10. Dependencies

To allow for efficient parallel processing, BitBake handles dependencies at the task level. Dependencies can exist both between tasks within a single recipe and between tasks in different recipes. Following are examples of each:

- For tasks within a single recipe, a recipe's do_configure task might need to complete before its do_compile task can run.

- For tasks in different recipes, one recipe's do_configure task might require another recipe's do_populate_sysroot task to finish first such that the libraries and headers provided by the other recipe are available.

This section describes several ways to declare dependencies. Remember, even though dependencies are declared in different ways, they are all simply dependencies between tasks.

3.10.1. Dependencies Internal to the **.bb** File

BitBake uses the addtask directive to manage dependencies that are internal to a given recipe file. You can use the addtask directive to indicate when a task is dependent on other tasks or when other tasks depend on that recipe. Here is an example:

```
addtask printdate after do_fetch before do_build
```

In this example, the do_printdate task depends on the completion of the do_fetch task, and the do_build task depends on the completion of the do_printdate task.

Note

For a task to run, it must be a direct or indirect dependency of some other task that is scheduled to run.

For illustration, here are some examples:

- The directive addtask mytask before do_configure causes do_mytask to run before do_configure runs. Be aware that do_mytask still only runs if its input checksum has changed since the last time it was run. Changes to the input checksum of do_mytask also indirectly cause do_configure to run.

- The directive addtask mytask after do_configure by itself never causes do_mytask to run. do_mytask can still be run manually as follows:

```
$ bitbake recipe -c mytask
```

Declaring do_mytask as a dependency of some other task that is scheduled to run also causes it to run. Regardless, the task runs after do_configure.

3.10.2. Build Dependencies

BitBake uses the DEPENDS variable to manage build time dependencies. The [deptask] varflag for tasks signifies the task of each item listed in DEPENDS that must complete before that task can be executed. Here is an example:

```
do_configure[deptask] = "do_populate_sysroot"
```

In this example, the do_populate_sysroot task of each item in DEPENDS must complete before do_configure can execute.

3.10.3. Runtime Dependencies

BitBake uses the PACKAGES, RDEPENDS, and RRECOMMENDS variables to manage runtime dependencies.

The PACKAGES variable lists runtime packages. Each of those packages can have RDEPENDS and RRECOMMENDS runtime dependencies. The [rdeptask] flag for tasks is used to signify the task of each item runtime dependency which must have completed before that task can be executed.

```
do_package_qa[rdeptask] = "do_packagedata"
```

In the previous example, the do_packagedata task of each item in RDEPENDS must have completed before do_package_qa can execute.

3.10.4. Recursive Dependencies

BitBake uses the [recrdeptask] flag to manage recursive task dependencies. BitBake looks through the build-time and runtime dependencies of the current recipe, looks through the task's inter-task dependencies, and then adds dependencies for the listed task. Once BitBake has accomplished this, it recursively works through the dependencies of those tasks. Iterative passes continue until all dependencies are discovered and added.

The [recrdeptask] flag is most commonly used in high-level recipes that need to wait for some task to finish "globally". For example, image.bbclass has the following:

```
do_rootfs[recrdeptask] += "do_packagedata"
```

This statement says that the do_packagedata task of the current recipe and all recipes reachable (by way of dependencies) from the image recipe must run before the do_rootfs task can run.

You might want to not only have BitBake look for dependencies of those tasks, but also have BitBake look for build-time and runtime dependencies of the dependent tasks as well. If that is the case, you need to reference the task name itself in the task list:

```
do_a[recrdeptask] = "do_a do_b"
```

3.10.5. Inter-Task Dependencies

BitBake uses the [depends] flag in a more generic form to manage inter-task dependencies. This more generic form allows for inter-dependency checks for specific tasks rather than checks for the data in DEPENDS. Here is an example:

```
do_patch[depends] = "quilt-native:do_populate_sysroot"
```

In this example, the do_populate_sysroot task of the target quilt-native must have completed before the do_patch task can execute.

The [rdepends] flag works in a similar way but takes targets in the runtime namespace instead of the build-time dependency namespace.

3.11. Functions You Can Call From Within Python

BitBake provides many functions you can call from within Python functions. This section lists the most commonly used functions, and mentions where to find others.

3.11.1. Functions for Accessing Datastore Variables

It is often necessary to access variables in the BitBake datastore using Python functions. The Bitbake datastore has an API that allows you this access. Here is a list of available operations:

Operation	Description
d.getVar("X", expand)	Returns the value of variable "X". Using "expand=True" expands the value. Returns "None" if the variable "X" does not exist.
d.setVar("X", "value")	Sets the variable "X" to "value".
d.appendVar("X", "value")	Adds "value" to the end of the variable "X". Acts like d.setVar("X", "value") if the variable "X" does not exist.

Operation	Description
d.prependVar("X", "value")	Adds "value" to the start of the variable "X". Acts like d.setVar("X", "value") if the variable "X" does not exist.
d.delVar("X")	Deletes the variable "X" from the datastore. Does nothing if the variable "X" does not exist.
d.renameVar("X", "Y")	Renames the variable "X" to "Y". Does nothing if the variable "X" does not exist.
d.getVarFlag("X", flag, expand)	Returns the value of variable "X". Using "expand=True" expands the value. Returns "None" if either the variable "X" or the named flag does not exist.
d.setVarFlag("X", flag, "value")	Sets the named flag for variable "X" to "value".
d.appendVarFlag("X", flag, "value")	Appends "value" to the named flag on the variable "X". Acts like d.setVarFlag("X", flag, "value") if the named flag does not exist.
d.prependVarFlag("X", flag, "value")	Prepends "value" to the named flag on the variable "X". Acts like d.setVarFlag("X", flag, "value") if the named flag does not exist.
d.delVarFlag("X", flag)	Deletes the named flag on the variable "X" from the datastore.
d.setVarFlags("X", flagsdict)	Sets the flags specified in the flagsdict() parameter. setVarFlags does not clear previous flags. Think of this operation as addVarFlags.
d.getVarFlags("X")	Returns a flagsdict of the flags for the variable "X". Returns "None" if the variable "X" does not exist.
d.delVarFlags("X")	Deletes all the flags for the variable "X". Does nothing if the variable "X" does not exist.
d.expand(expression)	Expands variable references in the specified string expression. References to variables that do not exist are left as is. For example, d.expand("foo ${X}") expands to the literal string "foo ${X}" if the variable "X" does not exist.

3.11.2. Other Functions

You can find many other functions that can be called from Python by looking at the source code of the bb module, which is in bitbake/lib/bb. For example, bitbake/lib/bb/utils.py includes the commonly used functions bb.utils.contains() and bb.utils.mkdirhier(), which come with docstrings.

3.12. Task Checksums and Setscene

BitBake uses checksums (or signatures) along with the setscene to determine if a task needs to be run. This section describes the process. To help understand how BitBake does this, the section assumes an OpenEmbedded metadata-based example.

This list is a place holder of content existed from previous work on the manual. Some or all of it probably needs integrated into the subsections that make up this section. For now, I have just provided a short glossary-like description for each variable. Ultimately, this list goes away.

• STAMP: The base path to create stamp files.

• STAMPCLEAN Again, the base path to create stamp files but can use wildcards for matching a range of files for clean operations.

- BB_STAMP_WHITELIST Lists stamp files that are looked at when the stamp policy is "whitelist".

- BB_STAMP_POLICY Defines the mode for comparing timestamps of stamp files.

- BB_HASHCHECK_FUNCTION Specifies the name of the function to call during the "setscene" part of the task's execution in order to validate the list of task hashes.

- BB_SETSCENE_VERIFY_FUNCTION2 Specifies a function to call that verifies the list of planned task execution before the main task execution happens.

- BB_SETSCENE_DEPVALID Specifies a function BitBake calls that determines whether BitBake requires a setscene dependency to be met.

- BB_TASKHASH Within an executing task, this variable holds the hash of the task as returned by the currently enabled signature generator.

Chapter 4. File Download Support

BitBake's fetch module is a standalone piece of library code that deals with the intricacies of downloading source code and files from remote systems. Fetching source code is one of the cornerstones of building software. As such, this module forms an important part of BitBake.

The current fetch module is called "fetch2" and refers to the fact that it is the second major version of the API. The original version is obsolete and has been removed from the codebase. Thus, in all cases, "fetch" refers to "fetch2" in this manual.

4.1. The Download (Fetch)

BitBake takes several steps when fetching source code or files. The fetcher codebase deals with two distinct processes in order: obtaining the files from somewhere (cached or otherwise) and then unpacking those files into a specific location and perhaps in a specific way. Getting and unpacking the files is often optionally followed by patching. Patching, however, is not covered by this module.

The code to execute the first part of this process, a fetch, looks something like the following:

```
src_uri = (d.getVar('SRC_URI') or "").split()
fetcher = bb.fetch2.Fetch(src_uri, d)
fetcher.download()
```

This code sets up an instance of the fetch class. The instance uses a space-separated list of URLs from the SRC_URI variable and then calls the download method to download the files.

The instantiation of the fetch class is usually followed by:

```
rootdir = l.getVar('WORKDIR')
fetcher.unpack(rootdir)
```

This code unpacks the downloaded files to the specified by WORKDIR.

> ## Note
> For convenience, the naming in these examples matches the variables used by OpenEmbedded. If you want to see the above code in action, examine the OpenEmbedded class file base.bbclass.

The SRC_URI and WORKDIR variables are not hardcoded into the fetcher, since those fetcher methods can be (and are) called with different variable names. In OpenEmbedded for example, the shared state (sstate) code uses the fetch module to fetch the sstate files.

When the download() method is called, BitBake tries to resolve the URLs by looking for source files in a specific search order:

• Pre-mirror Sites: BitBake first uses pre-mirrors to try and find source files. These locations are defined using the PREMIRRORS variable.

• Source URI: If pre-mirrors fail, BitBake uses the original URL (e.g from SRC_URI).

• Mirror Sites: If fetch failures occur, BitBake next uses mirror locations as defined by the MIRRORS variable.

For each URL passed to the fetcher, the fetcher calls the submodule that handles that particular URL type. This behavior can be the source of some confusion when you are providing URLs for the SRC_URI variable. Consider the following two URLs:

```
http://git.yoctoproject.org/git/poky;protocol=git
git://git.yoctoproject.org/git/poky;protocol=http
```

In the former case, the URL is passed to the wget fetcher, which does not understand "git". Therefore, the latter case is the correct form since the Git fetcher does know how to use HTTP as a transport.

Here are some examples that show commonly used mirror definitions:

```
PREMIRRORS ?= "\
    bzr://.*/.*    http://somemirror.org/sources/ \n \
    cvs://.*/.*    http://somemirror.org/sources/ \n \
    git://.*/.*    http://somemirror.org/sources/ \n \
    hg://.*/.*     http://somemirror.org/sources/ \n \
    osc://.*/.*    http://somemirror.org/sources/ \n \
    p4://.*/.*     http://somemirror.org/sources/ \n \
    svn://.*/.*    http://somemirror.org/sources/ \n"

MIRRORS =+ "\
    ftp://.*/.*      http://somemirror.org/sources/ \n \
    http://.*/.*     http://somemirror.org/sources/ \n \
    https://.*/.*    http://somemirror.org/sources/ \n"
```

It is useful to note that BitBake supports cross-URLs. It is possible to mirror a Git repository on an HTTP server as a tarball. This is what the git:// mapping in the previous example does.

Since network accesses are slow, Bitbake maintains a cache of files downloaded from the network. Any source files that are not local (i.e. downloaded from the Internet) are placed into the download directory, which is specified by the DL_DIR variable.

File integrity is of key importance for reproducing builds. For non-local archive downloads, the fetcher code can verify SHA-256 and MD5 checksums to ensure the archives have been downloaded correctly. You can specify these checksums by using the SRC_URI variable with the appropriate varflags as follows:

```
SRC_URI[md5sum] = "value"
SRC_URI[sha256sum] = "value"
```

You can also specify the checksums as parameters on the SRC_URI as shown below:

```
SRC_URI = "http://example.com/foobar.tar.bz2;md5sum=4a8e0f237e961fd7785d19d07fdb994d"
```

If multiple URIs exist, you can specify the checksums either directly as in the previous example, or you can name the URLs. The following syntax shows how you name the URIs:

```
SRC_URI = "http://example.com/foobar.tar.bz2;name=foo"
SRC_URI[foo.md5sum] = 4a8e0f237e961fd7785d19d07fdb994d
```

After a file has been downloaded and has had its checksum checked, a ".done" stamp is placed in DL_DIR. BitBake uses this stamp during subsequent builds to avoid downloading or comparing a checksum for the file again.

Note

It is assumed that local storage is safe from data corruption. If this were not the case, there would be bigger issues to worry about.

If BB_STRICT_CHECKSUM is set, any download without a checksum triggers an error message. The BB_NO_NETWORK variable can be used to make any attempted network access a fatal error, which is useful for checking that mirrors are complete as well as other things.

43

4.2. The Unpack

The unpack process usually immediately follows the download. For all URLs except Git URLs, BitBake uses the common unpack method.

A number of parameters exist that you can specify within the URL to govern the behavior of the unpack stage:

- unpack: Controls whether the URL components are unpacked. If set to "1", which is the default, the components are unpacked. If set to "0", the unpack stage leaves the file alone. This parameter is useful when you want an archive to be copied in and not be unpacked.

- dos: Applies to .zip and .jar files and specifies whether to use DOS line ending conversion on text files.

- basepath: Instructs the unpack stage to strip the specified directories from the source path when unpacking.

- subdir: Unpacks the specific URL to the specified subdirectory within the root directory.

The unpack call automatically decompresses and extracts files with ".Z", ".z", ".gz", ".xz", ".zip", ".jar", ".ipk", ".rpm". ".srpm", ".deb" and ".bz2" extensions as well as various combinations of tarball extensions.

As mentioned, the Git fetcher has its own unpack method that is optimized to work with Git trees. Basically, this method works by cloning the tree into the final directory. The process is completed using references so that there is only one central copy of the Git metadata needed.

4.3. Fetchers

As mentioned earlier, the URL prefix determines which fetcher submodule BitBake uses. Each submodule can support different URL parameters, which are described in the following sections.

4.3.1. Local file fetcher (`file://`)

This submodule handles URLs that begin with file://. The filename you specify within the URL can be either an absolute or relative path to a file. If the filename is relative, the contents of the FILESPATH variable is used in the same way PATH is used to find executables. If the file cannot be found, it is assumed that it is available in DL_DIR by the time the download() method is called.

If you specify a directory, the entire directory is unpacked.

Here are a couple of example URLs, the first relative and the second absolute:

```
SRC_URI = "file://relativefile.patch"
SRC_URI = "file:///Users/ich/very_important_software"
```

4.3.2. HTTP/FTP wget fetcher (`http://`, `ftp://`, `https://`)

This fetcher obtains files from web and FTP servers. Internally, the fetcher uses the wget utility.

The executable and parameters used are specified by the FETCHCMD_wget variable, which defaults to sensible values. The fetcher supports a parameter "downloadfilename" that allows the name of the downloaded file to be specified. Specifying the name of the downloaded file is useful for avoiding collisions in DL_DIR when dealing with multiple files that have the same name.

Some example URLs are as follows:

```
SRC_URI = "http://oe.handhelds.org/not_there.aac"
```

44

```
SRC_URI = "ftp://oe.handhelds.org/not_there_as_well.aac"
SRC_URI = "ftp://you@oe.handhelds.org/home/you/secret.plan"
```

Note

Because URL parameters are delimited by semi-colons, this can introduce ambiguity when parsing URLs that also contain semi-colons, for example:

```
SRC_URI = "http://abc123.org/git/?p=gcc/gcc.git;a=snapshot;h=a5dd47"
```

Such URLs should should be modified by replacing semi-colons with '&' characters:

```
SRC_URI = "http://abc123.org/git/?p=gcc/gcc.git&a=snapshot&h=a5dd47"
```

In most cases this should work. Treating semi-colons and '&' in queries identically is recommended by the World Wide Web Consortium (W3C). Note that due to the nature of the URL, you may have to specify the name of the downloaded file as well:

```
SRC_URI = "http://abc123.org/git/?p=gcc/gcc.git&a=snapshot&h=a5dd47;downloadfilename=
```

4.3.3. CVS fetcher (`cvs://`)

This submodule handles checking out files from the CVS version control system. You can configure it using a number of different variables:

- FETCHCMD_cvs: The name of the executable to use when running the cvs command. This name is usually "cvs".

- SRCDATE: The date to use when fetching the CVS source code. A special value of "now" causes the checkout to be updated on every build.

- CVSDIR: Specifies where a temporary checkout is saved. The location is often DL_DIR/cvs.

- CVS_PROXY_HOST: The name to use as a "proxy=" parameter to the cvs command.

- CVS_PROXY_PORT: The port number to use as a "proxyport=" parameter to the cvs command.

As well as the standard username and password URL syntax, you can also configure the fetcher with various URL parameters:

The supported parameters are as follows:

- "method": The protocol over which to communicate with the CVS server. By default, this protocol is "pserver". If "method" is set to "ext", BitBake examines the "rsh" parameter and sets CVS_RSH. You can use "dir" for local directories.

- "module": Specifies the module to check out. You must supply this parameter.

- "tag": Describes which CVS TAG should be used for the checkout. By default, the TAG is empty.

- "date": Specifies a date. If no "date" is specified, the SRCDATE of the configuration is used to checkout a specific date. The special value of "now" causes the checkout to be updated on every build.

- "localdir": Used to rename the module. Effectively, you are renaming the output directory to which the module is unpacked. You are forcing the module into a special directory relative to CVSDIR.

- "rsh" Used in conjunction with the "method" parameter.

- "scmdata": Causes the CVS metadata to be maintained in the tarball the fetcher creates when set to "keep". The tarball is expanded into the work directory. By default, the CVS metadata is removed.

- "fullpath": Controls whether the resulting checkout is at the module level, which is the default, or is at deeper paths.

- "norecurse": Causes the fetcher to only checkout the specified directory with no recurse into any subdirectories.

- "port": The port to which the CVS server connects.

Some example URLs are as follows:

```
SRC_URI = "cvs://CVSROOT;module=mymodule;tag=some-version;method=ext"
SRC_URI = "cvs://CVSROOT;module=mymodule;date=20060126;localdir=usethat"
```

4.3.4. Subversion (SVN) Fetcher (svn://)

This fetcher submodule fetches code from the Subversion source control system. The executable used is specified by FETCHCMD_svn, which defaults to "svn". The fetcher's temporary working directory is set by SVNDIR, which is usually DL_DIR/svn.

The supported parameters are as follows:

- "module": The name of the svn module to checkout. You must provide this parameter. You can think of this parameter as the top-level directory of the repository data you want.

- "path_spec": A specific directory in which to checkout the specified svn module.

- "protocol": The protocol to use, which defaults to "svn". If "protocol" is set to "svn+ssh", the "ssh" parameter is also used.

- "rev": The revision of the source code to checkout.

- "scmdata": Causes the ".svn" directories to be available during compile-time when set to "keep". By default, these directories are removed.

- "ssh": An optional parameter used when "protocol" is set to "svn+ssh". You can use this parameter to specify the ssh program used by svn.

- "transportuser": When required, sets the username for the transport. By default, this parameter is empty. The transport username is different than the username used in the main URL, which is passed to the subversion command.

Following are three examples using svn:

```
SRC_URI = "svn://myrepos/proj1;module=vip;protocol=http;rev=667"
SRC_URI = "svn://myrepos/proj1;module=opie;protocol=svn+ssh"
SRC_URI = "svn://myrepos/proj1;module=trunk;protocol=http;path_spec=${MY_DIR}/proj1"
```

4.3.5. Git Fetcher (git://)

This fetcher submodule fetches code from the Git source control system. The fetcher works by creating a bare clone of the remote into GITDIR, which is usually DL_DIR/git2. This bare clone is then cloned into the work directory during the unpack stage when a specific tree is checked out. This is done using alternates and by reference to minimize the amount of duplicate data on the disk and make the unpack process fast. The executable used can be set with FETCHCMD_git.

This fetcher supports the following parameters:

- "protocol": The protocol used to fetch the files. The default is "git" when a hostname is set. If a hostname is not set, the Git protocol is "file". You can also use "http", "https", "ssh" and "rsync".

- "nocheckout": Tells the fetcher to not checkout source code when unpacking when set to "1". Set this option for the URL where there is a custom routine to checkout code. The default is "0".

- "rebaseable": Indicates that the upstream Git repository can be rebased. You should set this parameter to "1" if revisions can become detached from branches. In this case, the source mirror tarball is done per revision, which has a loss of efficiency. Rebasing the upstream Git repository could cause the current revision to disappear from the upstream repository. This option reminds the fetcher to preserve the local cache carefully for future use. The default value for this parameter is "0".

- "nobranch": Tells the fetcher to not check the SHA validation for the branch when set to "1". The default is "0". Set this option for the recipe that refers to the commit that is valid for a tag instead of the branch.

- "bareclone": Tells the fetcher to clone a bare clone into the destination directory without checking out a working tree. Only the raw Git metadata is provided. This parameter implies the "nocheckout" parameter as well.

- "branch": The branch(es) of the Git tree to clone. If unset, this is assumed to be "master". The number of branch parameters much match the number of name parameters.

- "rev": The revision to use for the checkout. The default is "master".

- "tag": Specifies a tag to use for the checkout. To correctly resolve tags, BitBake must access the network. For that reason, tags are often not used. As far as Git is concerned, the "tag" parameter behaves effectively the same as the "rev" parameter.

- "subpath": Limits the checkout to a specific subpath of the tree. By default, the whole tree is checked out.

- "destsuffix": The name of the path in which to place the checkout. By default, the path is `git/`.

Here are some example URLs:

```
SRC_URI = "git://git.oe.handhelds.org/git/vip.git;tag=version-1"
SRC_URI = "git://git.oe.handhelds.org/git/vip.git;protocol=http"
```

4.3.6. Git Submodule Fetcher (`gitsm://`)

This fetcher submodule inherits from the Git fetcher and extends that fetcher's behavior by fetching a repository's submodules. SRC_URI is passed to the Git fetcher as described in the "Git Fetcher (`git://`)" section.

Notes and Warnings

You must clean a recipe when switching between '`git://`' and '`gitsm://`' URLs.

The Git Submodules fetcher is not a complete fetcher implementation. The fetcher has known issues where it does not use the normal source mirroring infrastructure properly. Further, the submodule sources it fetches are not visible to the licensing and source archiving infrastructures.

4.3.7. ClearCase Fetcher (`ccrc://`)

This fetcher submodule fetches code from a ClearCase [http://en.wikipedia.org/wiki/Rational_ClearCase] repository.

To use this fetcher, make sure your recipe has proper SRC_URI, SRCREV, and PV settings. Here is an example:

```
SRC_URI = "ccrc://cc.example.org/ccrc;vob=/example_vob;module=/example_module"
SRCREV = "EXAMPLE_CLEARCASE_TAG"
PV = "${@d.getVar("SRCREV", False).replace("/", "+")}"
```

The fetcher uses the `rcleartool` or `cleartool` remote client, depending on which one is available.

Following are options for the SRC_URI statement:

- vob: The name, which must include the prepending "/" character, of the ClearCase VOB. This option is required.

- module: The module, which must include the prepending "/" character, in the selected VOB.

Note

The module and vob options are combined to create the load rule in the view config spec. As an example, consider the vob and module values from the SRC_URI statement at the start of this section. Combining those values results in the following:

```
load /example_vob/example_module
```

- proto: The protocol, which can be either http or https.

By default, the fetcher creates a configuration specification. If you want this specification written to an area other than the default, use the CCASE_CUSTOM_CONFIG_SPEC variable in your recipe to define where the specification is written.

Note

the SRCREV loses its functionality if you specify this variable. However, SRCREV is still used to label the archive after a fetch even though it does not define what is fetched.

Here are a couple of other behaviors worth mentioning:

- When using cleartool, the login of cleartool is handled by the system. The login require no special steps.

- In order to use rcleartool with authenticated users, an "rcleartool login" is necessary before using the fetcher.

4.3.8. Perforce Fetcher (p4://)

This fetcher submodule fetches code from the Perforce [https://www.perforce.com/] source control system. The executable used is specified by FETCHCMD_p4, which defaults to "p4". The fetcher's temporary working directory is set by P4DIR, which defaults to "DL_DIR/p4".

To use this fetcher, make sure your recipe has proper SRC_URI, SRCREV, and PV values. The p4 executable is able to use the config file defined by your system's P4CONFIG environment variable in order to define the Perforce server URL and port, username, and password if you do not wish to keep those values in a recipe itself. If you choose not to use P4CONFIG, or to explicitly set variables that P4CONFIG can contain, you can specify the P4PORT value, which is the server's URL and port number, and you can specify a username and password directly in your recipe within SRC_URI.

Here is an example that relies on P4CONFIG to specify the server URL and port, username, and password, and fetches the Head Revision:

```
SRC_URI = "p4://example-depot/main/source/..."
SRCREV = "${AUTOREV}"
PV = "p4-${SRCPV}"
S = "${WORKDIR}/p4"
```

Here is an example that specifies the server URL and port, username, and password, and fetches a Revision based on a Label:

```
P4PORT = "tcp:p4server.example.net:1666"
SRC_URI = "p4://user:passwd@example-depot/main/source/..."
SRCREV = "release-1.0"
PV = "p4-${SRCPV}"
S = "${WORKDIR}/p4"
```

Note
You should always set S to "${WORKDIR}/p4" in your recipe.

4.3.9. Other Fetchers

Fetch submodules also exist for the following:

- Bazaar (`bzr://`)

- Trees using Git Annex (`gitannex://`)

- Secure FTP (`sftp://`)

- Secure Shell (`ssh://`)

- Repo (`repo://`)

- OSC (`osc://`)

- Mercurial (`hg://`)

No documentation currently exists for these lesser used fetcher submodules. However, you might find the code helpful and readable.

4.4. Auto Revisions

We need to document AUTOREV and SRCREV_FORMAT here.

Chapter 5. Variables Glossary

This chapter lists common variables used by BitBake and gives an overview of their function and contents.

Note

Following are some points regarding the variables listed in this glossary:

- The variables listed in this glossary are specific to BitBake. Consequently, the descriptions are limited to that context.

- Also, variables exist in other systems that use BitBake (e.g. The Yocto Project and OpenEmbedded) that have names identical to those found in this glossary. For such cases, the variables in those systems extend the functionality of the variable as it is described here in this glossary.

- Finally, there are variables mentioned in this glossary that do not appear in the BitBake glossary. These other variables are variables used in systems that use BitBake.

Glossary

A B C D E F G H L M O P R S T

A

ASSUME_PROVIDED

Lists recipe names (PN values) BitBake does not attempt to build. Instead, BitBake assumes these recipes have already been built.

In OpenEmbedded Core, ASSUME_PROVIDED mostly specifies native tools that should not be built. An example is git-native, which when specified allows for the Git binary from the host to be used rather than building git-native.

B

B

The directory in which BitBake executes functions during a recipe's build process.

BB_ALLOWED_NETWORKS

Specifies a space-delimited list of hosts that the fetcher is allowed to use to obtain the required source code. Following are considerations surrounding this variable:

- This host list is only used if BB_NO_NETWORK is either not set or set to "0".

- Limited support for wildcard matching against the beginning of host names exists. For example, the following setting matches git.gnu.org, ftp.gnu.org, and foo.git.gnu.org.

    BB_ALLOWED_NETWORKS = "*.gnu.org"

- Mirrors not in the host list are skipped and logged in debug.

- Attempts to access networks not in the host list cause a failure.

Using BB_ALLOWED_NETWORKS in conjunction with PREMIRRORS is very useful. Adding the host you want to use to PREMIRRORS results in the source code being fetched from an allowed location and avoids raising an error when a host that is not allowed is in a SRC_URI statement. This is because the fetcher does not attempt to use the host listed in SRC_URI after a successful fetch from the PREMIRRORS occurs.

BB_CONSOLELOG | Specifies the path to a log file into which BitBake's user interface writes output during the build.

BB_CURRENTTASK | Contains the name of the currently running task. The name does not include the do_ prefix.

BB_DANGLINGAPPENDS_WARNONLY | Defines how BitBake handles situations where an append file (.bbappend) has no corresponding recipe file (.bb). This condition often occurs when layers get out of sync (e.g. oe-core bumps a recipe version and the old recipe no longer exists and the other layer has not been updated to the new version of the recipe yet).

The default fatal behavior is safest because it is the sane reaction given something is out of sync. It is important to realize when your changes are no longer being applied.

BB_DEFAULT_TASK | The default task to use when none is specified (e.g. with the -c command line option). The task name specified should not include the do_ prefix.

BB_DISKMON_DIRS | Monitors disk space and available inodes during the build and allows you to control the build based on these parameters.

Disk space monitoring is disabled by default. When setting this variable, use the following form:

```
BB_DISKMON_DIRS = "<action>,<dir>,<threshold> [...]"
```

where:

```
<action> is:
    ABORT:      Immediately abort the build when
                a threshold is broken.
    STOPTASKS: Stop the build after the currently
                executing tasks have finished when
                a threshold is broken.
    WARN:       Issue a warning but continue the
                build when a threshold is broken.
                Subsequent warnings are issued as
                defined by the
                BB_DISKMON_WARNINTERVAL variable,
                which must be defined.

<dir> is:
    Any directory you choose. You can specify one or
    more directories to monitor by separating the
    groupings with a space.  If two directories are
    on the same device, only the first directory
    is monitored.

<threshold> is:
    Either the minimum available disk space,
    the minimum number of free inodes, or
    both.  You must specify at least one.  To
    omit one or the other, simply omit the value.
    Specify the threshold using G, M, K for Gbytes,
    Mbytes, and Kbytes, respectively. If you do
    not specify G, M, or K, Kbytes is assumed by
    default.  Do not use GB, MB, or KB.
```

Here are some examples:

51

```
BB_DISKMON_DIRS = "ABORT,${TMPDIR},1G,100K WARN,${SSTATE_DIR},1G,
BB_DISKMON_DIRS = "STOPTASKS,${TMPDIR},1G"
BB_DISKMON_DIRS = "ABORT,${TMPDIR},,100K"
```

The first example works only if you also set the BB_DISKMON_WARNINTERVAL variable. This example causes the build system to immediately abort when either the disk space in ${TMPDIR} drops below 1 Gbyte or the available free inodes drops below 100 Kbytes. Because two directories are provided with the variable, the build system also issues a warning when the disk space in the ${SSTATE_DIR} directory drops below 1 Gbyte or the number of free inodes drops below 100 Kbytes. Subsequent warnings are issued during intervals as defined by the BB_DISKMON_WARNINTERVAL variable.

The second example stops the build after all currently executing tasks complete when the minimum disk space in the ${TMPDIR} directory drops below 1 Gbyte. No disk monitoring occurs for the free inodes in this case.

The final example immediately aborts the build when the number of free inodes in the ${TMPDIR} directory drops below 100 Kbytes. No disk space monitoring for the directory itself occurs in this case.

BB_DISKMON_WARNINTERVAL   Defines the disk space and free inode warning intervals.

If you are going to use the BB_DISKMON_WARNINTERVAL variable, you must also use the BB_DISKMON_DIRS variable and define its action as "WARN". During the build, subsequent warnings are issued each time disk space or number of free inodes further reduces by the respective interval.

If you do not provide a BB_DISKMON_WARNINTERVAL variable and you do use BB_DISKMON_DIRS with the "WARN" action, the disk monitoring interval defaults to the following:

```
BB_DISKMON_WARNINTERVAL = "50M,5K"
```

When specifying the variable in your configuration file, use the following form:

```
BB_DISKMON_WARNINTERVAL = "<disk_space_interval>,<disk_inode_inte
```

where:

```
    <disk_space_interval> is:
        An interval of memory expressed in either
        G, M, or K for Gbytes, Mbytes, or Kbytes,
        respectively. You cannot use GB, MB, or KB.

    <disk_inode_interval> is:
        An interval of free inodes expressed in either
        G, M, or K for Gbytes, Mbytes, or Kbytes,
        respectively. You cannot use GB, MB, or KB.
```

Here is an example:

```
BB_DISKMON_DIRS = "WARN,${SSTATE_DIR},1G,100K"
```

$$BB\_DISKMON\_WARNINTERVAL = "50M,5K"$$

These variables cause BitBake to issue subsequent warnings each time the available disk space further reduces by 50 Mbytes or the number of free inodes further reduces by 5 Kbytes in the ${SSTATE_DIR} directory. Subsequent warnings based on the interval occur each time a respective interval is reached beyond the initial warning (i.e. 1 Gbytes and 100 Kbytes).

BB_ENV_WHITELIST   Specifies the internal whitelist of variables to allow through from the external environment into BitBake's datastore. If the value of this variable is not specified (which is the default), the following list is used: BBPATH, BB_PRESERVE_ENV, BB_ENV_WHITELIST, and BB_ENV_EXTRAWHITE.

Note

You must set this variable in the external environment in order for it to work.

BB_ENV_EXTRAWHITE   Specifies an additional set of variables to allow through (whitelist) from the external environment into BitBake's datastore. This list of variables are on top of the internal list set in BB_ENV_WHITELIST.

Note

You must set this variable in the external environment in order for it to work.

BB_FETCH_PREMIRRORONLY   When set to "1", causes BitBake's fetcher module to only search PREMIRRORS for files. BitBake will not search the main SRC_URI or MIRRORS.

BB_FILENAME   Contains the filename of the recipe that owns the currently running task. For example, if the do_fetch task that resides in the my-recipe.bb is executing, the BB_FILENAME variable contains "/foo/path/my-recipe.bb".

BB_GENERATE_MIRROR_TARBALLS   Causes tarballs of the Git repositories, including the Git metadata, to be placed in the DL_DIR directory. Anyone wishing to create a source mirror would want to enable this variable.

For performance reasons, creating and placing tarballs of the Git repositories is not the default action by BitBake.

$$BB\_GENERATE\_MIRROR\_TARBALLS = "1"$$

BB_HASHCONFIG_WHITELIST   Lists variables that are excluded from base configuration checksum, which is used to determine if the cache can be reused.

One of the ways BitBake determines whether to re-parse the main metadata is through checksums of the variables in the datastore of the base configuration data. There are variables that you typically want to exclude when checking whether or not to re-parse and thus rebuild the cache. As an example, you would usually exclude TIME and DATE because these variables are always changing. If you did not exclude them, BitBake would never reuse the cache.

BB_HASHBASE_WHITELIST   Lists variables that are excluded from checksum and dependency data. Variables that are excluded can therefore change without affecting the checksum mechanism. A common example would be the variable for the path of the build. BitBake's output should not (and usually does not) depend on the directory in which it was built.

BB_HASHCHECK_FUNCTION	Specifies the name of the function to call during the "setscene" part of the task's execution in order to validate the list of task hashes. The function returns the list of setscene tasks that should be executed.

At this point in the execution of the code, the objective is to quickly verify if a given setscene function is likely to work or not. It's easier to check the list of setscene functions in one pass than to call many individual tasks. The returned list need not be completely accurate. A given setscene task can still later fail. However, the more accurate the data returned, the more efficient the build will be. |
| BB_INVALIDCONF | Used in combination with the ConfigParsed event to trigger re-parsing the base metadata (i.e. all the recipes). The ConfigParsed event can set the variable to trigger the re-parse. You must be careful to avoid recursive loops with this functionality. |
| BB_LOGFMT | Specifies the name of the log files saved into ${T}. By default, the BB_LOGFMT variable is undefined and the log file names get created using the following form:

    `log.{task}.{pid}`

If you want to force log files to take a specific name, you can set this variable in a configuration file. |
| BB_NICE_LEVEL | Allows BitBake to run at a specific priority (i.e. nice level). System permissions usually mean that BitBake can reduce its priority but not raise it again. See BB_TASK_NICE_LEVEL for additional information. |
| BB_NO_NETWORK | Disables network access in the BitBake fetcher modules. With this access disabled, any command that attempts to access the network becomes an error.

Disabling network access is useful for testing source mirrors, running builds when not connected to the Internet, and when operating in certain kinds of firewall environments. |
| BB_NUMBER_THREADS | The maximum number of tasks BitBake should run in parallel at any one time. If your host development system supports multiple cores, a good rule of thumb is to set this variable to twice the number of cores. |
| BB_NUMBER_PARSE_THREADS | Sets the number of threads BitBake uses when parsing. By default, the number of threads is equal to the number of cores on the system. |
| BB_ORIGENV | Contains a copy of the original external environment in which BitBake was run. The copy is taken before any whitelisted variable values are filtered into BitBake's datastore.

Note
The contents of this variable is a datastore object that can be queried using the normal datastore operations. |
| BB_PRESERVE_ENV | Disables whitelisting and instead allows all variables through from the external environment into BitBake's datastore.

Note
You must set this variable in the external environment in order for it to work. |
| BB_RUNFMT | Specifies the name of the executable script files (i.e. run files) saved into ${T}. By default, the BB_RUNFMT variable is undefined and the run file names get created using the following form: |

```
run.{task}.{pid}
```

If you want to force run files to take a specific name, you can set this variable in a configuration file.

BB_RUNTASK	Contains the name of the currently executing task. The value does not include the "do_" prefix. For example, if the currently executing task is do_config, the value is "config".
BB_SCHEDULER	Selects the name of the scheduler to use for the scheduling of BitBake tasks. Three options exist:

- basic - The basic framework from which everything derives. Using this option causes tasks to be ordered numerically as they are parsed.

- speed - Executes tasks first that have more tasks depending on them. The "speed" option is the default.

- completion - Causes the scheduler to try to complete a given recipe once its build has started.

BB_SCHEDULERS	Defines custom schedulers to import. Custom schedulers need to be derived from the RunQueueScheduler class.

For information how to select a scheduler, see the BB_SCHEDULER variable.

BB_SETSCENE_DEPVALID	Specifies a function BitBake calls that determines whether BitBake requires a setscene dependency to be met.

When running a setscene task, BitBake needs to know which dependencies of that setscene task also need to be run. Whether dependencies also need to be run is highly dependent on the metadata. The function specified by this variable returns a "True" or "False" depending on whether the dependency needs to be met.

BB_SETSCENE_VERIFY_FUNCTION2 Specifies a function to call that verifies the list of planned task execution before the main task execution happens. The function is called once BitBake has a list of setscene tasks that have run and either succeeded or failed.

The function allows for a task list check to see if they make sense. Even if BitBake was planning to skip a task, the returned value of the function can force BitBake to run the task, which is necessary under certain metadata defined circumstances.

BB_SIGNATURE_EXCLUDE_FLAGS Lists variable flags (varflags) that can be safely excluded from checksum and dependency data for keys in the datastore. When generating checksum or dependency data for keys in the datastore, the flags set against that key are normally included in the checksum.

For more information on varflags, see the "Variable Flags" section.

BB_SIGNATURE_HANDLER	Defines the name of the signature handler BitBake uses. The signature handler defines the way stamp files are created and handled, if and how the signature is incorporated into the stamps, and how the signature itself is generated.

A new signature handler can be added by injecting a class derived from the SignatureGenerator class into the global namespace.

BB_SRCREV_POLICY	Defines the behavior of the fetcher when it interacts with source control systems and dynamic source revisions. The BB_SRCREV_POLICY variable is useful when working without a network.

The variable can be set using one of two policies:

- cache - Retains the value the system obtained previously rather than querying the source control system each time.

- clear - Queries the source controls system every time. With this policy, there is no cache. The "clear" policy is the default.

BB_STAMP_POLICY   Defines the mode used for how timestamps of stamp files are compared. You can set the variable to one of the following modes:

- perfile - Timestamp comparisons are only made between timestamps of a specific recipe. This is the default mode.

- full - Timestamp comparisons are made for all dependencies.

- whitelist - Identical to "full" mode except timestamp comparisons are made for recipes listed in the BB_STAMP_WHITELIST variable.

Note
Stamp policies are largely obsolete with the introduction of setscene tasks.

BB_STAMP_WHITELIST   Lists files whose stamp file timestamps are compared when the stamp policy mode is set to "whitelist". For information on stamp policies, see the BB_STAMP_POLICY variable.

BB_STRICT_CHECKSUM   Sets a more strict checksum mechanism for non-local URLs. Setting this variable to a value causes BitBake to report an error if it encounters a non-local URL that does not have at least one checksum specified.

BB_TASK_IONICE_LEVEL   Allows adjustment of a task's Input/Output priority. During Autobuilder testing, random failures can occur for tasks due to I/O starvation. These failures occur during various QEMU runtime timeouts. You can use the BB_TASK_IONICE_LEVEL variable to adjust the I/O priority of these tasks.

Note
This variable works similarly to the BB_TASK_NICE_LEVEL variable except with a task's I/O priorities.

Set the variable as follows:

```
BB_TASK_IONICE_LEVEL = "class.prio"
```

For class, the default value is "2", which is a best effort. You can use "1" for realtime and "3" for idle. If you want to use realtime, you must have superuser privileges.

For prio, you can use any value from "0", which is the highest priority, to "7", which is the lowest. The default value is "4". You do not need any special privileges to use this range of priority values.

Note
In order for your I/O priority settings to take effect, you need the Completely Fair Queuing (CFQ) Scheduler selected for the backing block device. To select the scheduler, use the following command form where device is the device (e.g. sda, sdb, and so forth):

```
$ sudo sh -c "echo cfq > /sys/block/device/queu/scheduler
```

BB_TASK_NICE_LEVEL	Allows specific tasks to change their priority (i.e. nice level).

You can use this variable in combination with task overrides to raise or lower priorities of specific tasks. For example, on the Yocto Project [http://www.yoctoproject.org] autobuilder, QEMU emulation in images is given a higher priority as compared to build tasks to ensure that images do not suffer timeouts on loaded systems.

BB_TASKHASH	Within an executing task, this variable holds the hash of the task as returned by the currently enabled signature generator.
BB_VERBOSE_LOGS	Controls how verbose BitBake is during builds. If set, shell scripts echo commands and shell script output appears on standard out (stdout).
BB_WORKERCONTEXT	Specifies if the current context is executing a task. BitBake sets this variable to "1" when a task is being executed. The value is not set when the task is in server context during parsing or event handling.
BBCLASSEXTEND	Allows you to extend a recipe so that it builds variants of the software. Some examples of these variants for recipes from the OpenEmbedded Core metadata are "natives" such as quilt-native, which is a copy of Quilt built to run on the build system; "crosses" such as gcc-cross, which is a compiler built to run on the build machine but produces binaries that run on the target MACHINE; "nativesdk", which targets the SDK machine instead of MACHINE; and "mulitlibs" in the form "multilib:multilib_name".

To build a different variant of the recipe with a minimal amount of code, it usually is as simple as adding the variable to your recipe. Here are two examples. The "native" variants are from the OpenEmbedded Core metadata:

```
BBCLASSEXTEND =+ "native nativesdk"
BBCLASSEXTEND =+ "multilib:multilib_name"
```

Note

Internally, the BBCLASSEXTEND mechanism generates recipe variants by rewriting variable values and applying overrides such as _class-native. For example, to generate a native version of a recipe, a DEPENDS on "foo" is rewritten to a DEPENDS on "foo-native".

Even when using BBCLASSEXTEND, the recipe is only parsed once. Parsing once adds some limitations. For example, it is not possible to include a different file depending on the variant, since include statements are processed when the recipe is parsed.

BBDEBUG	Sets the BitBake debug output level to a specific value as incremented by the -D command line option.

Note
You must set this variable in the external environment in order for it to work.

BBFILE_COLLECTIONS	Lists the names of configured layers. These names are used to find the other BBFILE_* variables. Typically, each layer appends its name to this variable in its conf/layer.conf file.
BBFILE_PATTERN	Variable that expands to match files from BBFILES in a particular layer. This variable is used in the conf/layer.conf file and

must be suffixed with the name of the specific layer (e.g. BBFILE_PATTERN_emenlow).

BBFILE_PRIORITY

Assigns the priority for recipe files in each layer.

This variable is useful in situations where the same recipe appears in more than one layer. Setting this variable allows you to prioritize a layer against other layers that contain the same recipe - effectively letting you control the precedence for the multiple layers. The precedence established through this variable stands regardless of a recipe's version (PV variable). For example, a layer that has a recipe with a higher PV value but for which the BBFILE_PRIORITY is set to have a lower precedence still has a lower precedence.

A larger value for the BBFILE_PRIORITY variable results in a higher precedence. For example, the value 6 has a higher precedence than the value 5. If not specified, the BBFILE_PRIORITY variable is set based on layer dependencies (see the LAYERDEPENDS variable for more information. The default priority, if unspecified for a layer with no dependencies, is the lowest defined priority + 1 (or 1 if no priorities are defined).

Tip

You can use the command `bitbake-layers show-layers` to list all configured layers along with their priorities.

BBFILES

List of recipe files BitBake uses to build software.

BBINCLUDED

Contains a space-separated list of all of all files that BitBake's parser included during parsing of the current file.

BBINCLUDELOGS

If set to a value, enables printing the task log when reporting a failed task.

BBINCLUDELOGS_LINES

If BBINCLUDELOGS is set, specifies the maximum number of lines from the task log file to print when reporting a failed task. If you do not set BBINCLUDELOGS_LINES, the entire log is printed.

BBLAYERS

Lists the layers to enable during the build. This variable is defined in the `bblayers.conf` configuration file in the build directory. Here is an example:

```
BBLAYERS = " \
    /home/scottrif/poky/meta \
    /home/scottrif/poky/meta-yocto \
    /home/scottrif/poky/meta-yocto-bsp \
    /home/scottrif/poky/meta-mykernel \
    "
```

This example enables four layers, one of which is a custom, user-defined layer named `meta-mykernel`.

BBLAYERS_FETCH_DIR

Sets the base location where layers are stored. This setting is used in conjunction with `bitbake-layers layerindex-fetch` and tells `bitbake-layers` where to place the fetched layers.

BBMASK

Prevents BitBake from processing recipes and recipe append files.

You can use the BBMASK variable to "hide" these .bb and .bbappend files. BitBake ignores any recipe or recipe append files that match any of the expressions. It is as if BitBake does not see them at all. Consequently, matching files are not parsed or otherwise used by BitBake.

The values you provide are passed to Python's regular expression compiler. The expressions are compared against the full paths to the files. For complete syntax information, see Python's documentation at http://docs.python.org/release/2.3/lib/re-syntax.html.

The following example uses a complete regular expression to tell BitBake to ignore all recipe and recipe append files in the meta-ti/ recipes-misc/ directory:

```
BBMASK = "meta-ti/recipes-misc/"
```

If you want to mask out multiple directories or recipes, you can specify multiple regular expression fragments. This next example masks out multiple directories and individual recipes:

```
BBMASK += "/meta-ti/recipes-misc/ meta-ti/recipes-ti/packagegr
BBMASK += "/meta-oe/recipes-support/"
BBMASK += "/meta-foo/.*/openldap"
BBMASK += "opencv.*\.bbappend"
BBMASK += "lzma"
```

Note
When specifying a directory name, use the trailing slash character to ensure you match just that directory name.

BBPATH

Used by BitBake to locate class (.bbclass) and configuration (.conf) files. This variable is analogous to the PATH variable.

If you run BitBake from a directory outside of the build directory, you must be sure to set BBPATH to point to the build directory. Set the variable as you would any environment variable and then run BitBake:

```
$ BBPATH="build_directory"
$ export BBPATH
$ bitbake target
```

BBSERVER

Points to the server that runs memory-resident BitBake. The variable is only used when you employ memory-resident BitBake.

BBTARGETS

Allows you to use a configuration file to add to the list of command-line target recipes you want to build.

BBVERSIONS

Allows a single recipe to build multiple versions of a project from a single recipe file. You also able to specify conditional metadata using the OVERRIDES mechanism for a single version or for an optionally named range of versions.

For more information on BBVERSIONS, see the "Variants - Class Extension Mechanism" section.

BITBAKE_UI

Used to specify the UI module to use when running BitBake. Using this variable is equivalent to using the -u command-line option.

Note
You must set this variable in the external environment in order for it to work.

BUILDNAME

A name assigned to the build. The name defaults to a datetime stamp of when the build was started but can be defined by the metadata.

BZRDIR	The directory in which files checked out of a Bazaar system are stored.

C

CACHE	Specifies the directory BitBake uses to store a cache of the metadata so it does not need to be parsed every time BitBake is started.
CVSDIR	The directory in which files checked out under the CVS system are stored.

D

DEFAULT_PREFERENCE

Specifies a weak bias for recipe selection priority.

The most common usage of this is variable is to set it to "-1" within a recipe for a development version of a piece of software. Using the variable in this way causes the stable version of the recipe to build by default in the absence of PREFERRED_VERSION being used to build the development version.

> ## Note
> The bias provided by DEFAULT_PREFERENCE is weak and is overridden by BBFILE_PRIORITY if that variable is different between two layers that contain different versions of the same recipe.

DEPENDS

Lists a recipe's build-time dependencies (i.e. other recipe files).

Consider this simple example for two recipes named "a" and "b" that produce similarly named packages. In this example, the DEPENDS statement appears in the "a" recipe:

```
DEPENDS = "b"
```

Here, the dependency is such that the do_configure task for recipe "a" depends on the do_populate_sysroot task of recipe "b". This means anything that recipe "b" puts into sysroot is available when recipe "a" is configuring itself.

For information on runtime dependencies, see the RDEPENDS variable.

DESCRIPTION	A long description for the recipe.
DL_DIR	The central download directory used by the build process to store downloads. By default, DL_DIR gets files suitable for mirroring for everything except Git repositories. If you want tarballs of Git repositories, use the BB_GENERATE_MIRROR_TARBALLS variable.

E

EXCLUDE_FROM_WORLD

Directs BitBake to exclude a recipe from world builds (i.e. bitbake world). During world builds, BitBake locates, parses and builds all recipes found in every layer exposed in the bblayers.conf configuration file.

To exclude a recipe from a world build using this variable, set the variable to "1" in the recipe.

> ## Note
> Recipes added to EXCLUDE_FROM_WORLD may still be built during a world build in order to satisfy dependencies of

other recipes. Adding a recipe to EXCLUDE_FROM_WORLD only ensures that the recipe is not explicitly added to the list of build targets in a world build.

F

FAKEROOT	Contains the command to use when running a shell script in a fakeroot environment. The FAKEROOT variable is obsolete and has been replaced by the other FAKEROOT* variables. See these entries in the glossary for more information.
FAKEROOTBASEENV	Lists environment variables to set when executing the command defined by FAKEROOTCMD that starts the bitbake-worker process in the fakeroot environment.
FAKEROOTCMD	Contains the command that starts the bitbake-worker process in the fakeroot environment.
FAKEROOTDIRS	Lists directories to create before running a task in the fakeroot environment.
FAKEROOTENV	Lists environment variables to set when running a task in the fakeroot environment. For additional information on environment variables and the fakeroot environment, see the FAKEROOTBASEENV variable.
FAKEROOTNOENV	Lists environment variables to set when running a task that is not in the fakeroot environment. For additional information on environment variables and the fakeroot environment, see the FAKEROOTENV variable.
FETCHCMD	Defines the command the BitBake fetcher module executes when running fetch operations. You need to use an override suffix when you use the variable (e.g. FETCHCMD_git or FETCHCMD_svn).
FILE	Points at the current file. BitBake sets this variable during the parsing process to identify the file being parsed. BitBake also sets this variable when a recipe is being executed to identify the recipe file.
FILESPATH	Specifies directories BitBake uses when searching for patches and files. The "local" fetcher module uses these directories when handling file:// URLs. The variable behaves like a shell PATH environment variable. The value is a colon-separated list of directories that are searched left-to-right in order.

G

GITDIR	The directory in which a local copy of a Git repository is stored when it is cloned.

H

HGDIR	The directory in which files checked out of a Mercurial system are stored.
HOMEPAGE	Website where more information about the software the recipe is building can be found.

I

INHERIT	Causes the named class or classes to be inherited globally. Anonymous functions in the class or classes are not executed for the base configuration and in each individual recipe. The OpenEmbedded build system ignores changes to INHERIT in individual recipes.

For more information on INHERIT, see the "INHERIT Configuration Directive" section.

L

LAYERDEPENDS
Lists the layers, separated by spaces, upon which this recipe depends. Optionally, you can specify a specific layer version for a dependency by adding it to the end of the layer name with a colon, (e.g. "anotherlayer:3" to be compared against LAYERVERSION_anotherlayer in this case). BitBake produces an error if any dependency is missing or the version numbers do not match exactly (if specified).

You use this variable in the conf/layer.conf file. You must also use the specific layer name as a suffix to the variable (e.g. LAYERDEPENDS_mylayer).

LAYERDIR
When used inside the layer.conf configuration file, this variable provides the path of the current layer. This variable is not available outside of layer.conf and references are expanded immediately when parsing of the file completes.

LAYERDIR_RE
When used inside the layer.conf configuration file, this variable provides the path of the current layer, escaped for use in a regular expression (BBFILE_PATTERN). This variable is not available outside of layer.conf and references are expanded immediately when parsing of the file completes.

LAYERVERSION
Optionally specifies the version of a layer as a single number. You can use this variable within LAYERDEPENDS for another layer in order to depend on a specific version of the layer.

You use this variable in the conf/layer.conf file. You must also use the specific layer name as a suffix to the variable (e.g. LAYERDEPENDS_mylayer).

LICENSE
The list of source licenses for the recipe.

M

MIRRORS
Specifies additional paths from which BitBake gets source code. When the build system searches for source code, it first tries the local download directory. If that location fails, the build system tries locations defined by PREMIRRORS, the upstream source, and then locations specified by MIRRORS in that order.

MULTI_PROVIDER_WHITELIST
Allows you to suppress BitBake warnings caused when building two separate recipes that provide the same output.

Bitbake normally issues a warning when building two different recipes where each provides the same output. This scenario is usually something the user does not want. However, cases do exist where it makes sense, particularly in the virtual/* namespace. You can use this variable to suppress BitBake's warnings.

To use the variable, list provider names (e.g. recipe names, virtual/kernel, and so forth).

O

OVERRIDES
BitBake uses OVERRIDES to control what variables are overridden after BitBake parses recipes and configuration files.

Following is a simple example that uses an overrides list based on machine architectures:

```
OVERRIDES = "arm:x86:mips:powerpc"
```

You can find information on how to use OVERRIDES in the "Conditional Syntax (Overrides)" section.

P

P4DIR

The directory in which a local copy of a Perforce depot is stored when it is fetched.

PACKAGES

The list of packages the recipe creates.

PACKAGES_DYNAMIC

A promise that your recipe satisfies runtime dependencies for optional modules that are found in other recipes. PACKAGES_DYNAMIC does not actually satisfy the dependencies, it only states that they should be satisfied. For example, if a hard, runtime dependency (RDEPENDS) of another package is satisfied during the build through the PACKAGES_DYNAMIC variable, but a package with the module name is never actually produced, then the other package will be broken.

PE

The epoch of the recipe. By default, this variable is unset. The variable is used to make upgrades possible when the versioning scheme changes in some backwards incompatible way.

PERSISTENT_DIR

Specifies the directory BitBake uses to store data that should be preserved between builds. In particular, the data stored is the data that uses BitBake's persistent data API and the data used by the PR Server and PR Service.

PF

Specifies the recipe or package name and includes all version and revision numbers (i.e. `eglibc-2.13-r20+svnr15508/` and `bash-4.2-r1/`).

PN

The recipe name.

PR

The revision of the recipe.

PREFERRED_PROVIDER

Determines which recipe should be given preference when multiple recipes provide the same item. You should always suffix the variable with the name of the provided item, and you should set it to the PN of the recipe to which you want to give precedence. Some examples:

```
PREFERRED_PROVIDER_virtual/kernel ?= "linux-yocto"
PREFERRED_PROVIDER_virtual/xserver = "xserver-xf86"
PREFERRED_PROVIDER_virtual/libgl ?= "mesa"
```

PREFERRED_PROVIDERS

Determines which recipe should be given preference for cases where multiple recipes provide the same item. Functionally, PREFERRED_PROVIDERS is identical to PREFERRED_PROVIDER. However, the PREFERRED_PROVIDERS variable lets you define preferences for multiple situations using the following form:

```
PREFERRED_PROVIDERS = "xxx:yyy aaa:bbb ..."
```

This form is a convenient replacement for the following:

63

```
PREFERRED_PROVIDER_xxx = "yyy"
PREFERRED_PROVIDER_aaa = "bbb"
```

PREFERRED_VERSION

If there are multiple versions of recipes available, this variable determines which recipe should be given preference. You must always suffix the variable with the PN you want to select, and you should set PV accordingly for precedence. You can use the "%" character as a wildcard to match any number of characters, which can be useful when specifying versions that contain long revision numbers that could potentially change. Here are two examples:

```
PREFERRED_VERSION_python = "2.7.3"
PREFERRED_VERSION_linux-yocto = "4.12%"
```

PREMIRRORS

Specifies additional paths from which BitBake gets source code. When the build system searches for source code, it first tries the local download directory. If that location fails, the build system tries locations defined by PREMIRRORS, the upstream source, and then locations specified by MIRRORS in that order.

Typically, you would add a specific server for the build system to attempt before any others by adding something like the following to your configuration:

```
PREMIRRORS_prepend = "\
git://.*/.* http://www.yoctoproject.org/sources/ \n \
ftp://.*/.* http://www.yoctoproject.org/sources/ \n \
http://.*/.* http://www.yoctoproject.org/sources/ \n \
https://.*/.* http://www.yoctoproject.org/sources/ \n"
```

These changes cause the build system to intercept Git, FTP, HTTP, and HTTPS requests and direct them to the http:// sources mirror. You can use file:// URLs to point to local directories or network shares as well.

PROVIDES

A list of aliases by which a particular recipe can be known. By default, a recipe's own PN is implicitly already in its PROVIDES list. If a recipe uses PROVIDES, the additional aliases are synonyms for the recipe and can be useful satisfying dependencies of other recipes during the build as specified by DEPENDS.

Consider the following example PROVIDES statement from a recipe file libav_0.8.11.bb:

```
PROVIDES += "libpostproc"
```

The PROVIDES statement results in the "libav" recipe also being known as "libpostproc".

In addition to providing recipes under alternate names, the PROVIDES mechanism is also used to implement virtual targets. A virtual target is a name that corresponds to some particular functionality (e.g. a Linux kernel). Recipes that provide the functionality in question list the virtual target in PROVIDES. Recipes that depend on the functionality in question can include the virtual target in DEPENDS to leave the choice of provider open.

Conventionally, virtual targets have names on the form "virtual/function" (e.g. "virtual/kernel"). The slash is simply part of the name and has no syntactical significance.

PRSERV_HOST

The network based PR service host and port.

Following is an example of how the PRSERV_HOST variable is set:

```
PRSERV_HOST = "localhost:0"
```

You must set the variable if you want to automatically start a local PR service. You can set PRSERV_HOST to other values to use a remote PR service.

PV

The version of the recipe.

R

RDEPENDS

Lists a package's runtime dependencies (i.e. other packages) that must be installed in order for the built package to run correctly. If a package in this list cannot be found during the build, you will get a build error.

Because the RDEPENDS variable applies to packages being built, you should always use the variable in a form with an attached package name. For example, suppose you are building a development package that depends on the perl package. In this case, you would use the following RDEPENDS statement:

```
RDEPENDS_${PN}-dev += "perl"
```

In the example, the development package depends on the perl package. Thus, the RDEPENDS variable has the ${PN}-dev package name as part of the variable.

BitBake supports specifying versioned dependencies. Although the syntax varies depending on the packaging format, BitBake hides these differences from you. Here is the general syntax to specify versions with the RDEPENDS variable:

```
RDEPENDS_${PN} = "package (operator version)"
```

For operator, you can specify the following:

```
=
<
>
<=
>=
```

For example, the following sets up a dependency on version 1.2 or greater of the package foo:

```
RDEPENDS_${PN} = "foo (>= 1.2)"
```

For information on build-time dependencies, see the DEPENDS variable.

RPROVIDES

A list of package name aliases that a package also provides. These aliases are useful for satisfying runtime dependencies of other packages both during the build and on the target (as specified by RDEPENDS).

As with all package-controlling variables, you must always use the variable in conjunction with a package name override. Here is an example:

```
RPROVIDES_${PN} = "widget-abi-2"
```

RRECOMMENDS

A list of packages that extends the usability of a package being built. The package being built does not depend on this list of packages in order to successfully build, but needs them for the extended usability. To specify runtime dependencies for packages, see the RDEPENDS variable.

BitBake supports specifying versioned recommends. Although the syntax varies depending on the packaging format, BitBake hides these differences from you. Here is the general syntax to specify versions with the RRECOMMENDS variable:

```
RRECOMMENDS_${PN} = "package (operator version)"
```

For operator, you can specify the following:

```
=
<
>
<=
>=
```

For example, the following sets up a recommend on version 1.2 or greater of the package foo:

```
RRECOMMENDS_${PN} = "foo (>= 1.2)"
```

S

SECTION

The section in which packages should be categorized.

SRC_URI

The list of source files - local or remote. This variable tells BitBake which bits to pull for the build and how to pull them. For example, if the recipe or append file needs to fetch a single tarball from the Internet, the recipe or append file uses a SRC_URI entry that specifies that tarball. On the other hand, if the recipe or append file needs to fetch a tarball and include a custom file, the recipe or append file needs an SRC_URI variable that specifies all those sources.

The following list explains the available URI protocols:

- file:// - Fetches files, which are usually files shipped with the metadata, from the local machine. The path is relative to the FILESPATH variable.

- bzr:// - Fetches files from a Bazaar revision control repository.

- git:// - Fetches files from a Git revision control repository.

- `osc://` - Fetches files from an OSC (OpenSUSE Build service) revision control repository.

- `repo://` - Fetches files from a repo (Git) repository.

- `http://` - Fetches files from the Internet using HTTP.

- `https://` - Fetches files from the Internet using HTTPS.

- `ftp://` - Fetches files from the Internet using FTP.

- `cvs://` - Fetches files from a CVS revision control repository.

- `hg://` - Fetches files from a Mercurial (hg) revision control repository.

- `p4://` - Fetches files from a Perforce (p4) revision control repository.

- `ssh://` - Fetches files from a secure shell.

- `svn://` - Fetches files from a Subversion (svn) revision control repository.

Here are some additional options worth mentioning:

- `unpack` - Controls whether or not to unpack the file if it is an archive. The default action is to unpack the file.

- `subdir` - Places the file (or extracts its contents) into the specified subdirectory. This option is useful for unusual tarballs or other archives that do not have their files already in a subdirectory within the archive.

- `name` - Specifies a name to be used for association with SRC_URI checksums when you have more than one file specified in SRC_URI.

- `downloadfilename` - Specifies the filename used when storing the downloaded file.

SRCDATE	The date of the source code used to build the package. This variable applies only if the source was fetched from a Source Code Manager (SCM).
SRCREV	The revision of the source code used to build the package. This variable applies only when using Subversion, Git, Mercurial and Bazaar. If you want to build a fixed revision and you want to avoid performing a query on the remote repository every time BitBake parses your recipe, you should specify a SRCREV that is a full revision identifier and not just a tag.
SRCREV_FORMAT	Helps construct valid SRCREV values when multiple source controlled URLs are used in SRC_URI. The system needs help constructing these values under these circumstances. Each component in the SRC_URI is assigned a name and these are referenced in the SRCREV_FORMAT variable. Consider an example with URLs named "machine" and "meta". In this case, SRCREV_FORMAT could look like "machine_meta" and those names would have the SCM versions substituted into each position. Only one AUTOINC placeholder is added and if needed. And, this placeholder is placed at the start of the returned string.
STAMP	Specifies the base path used to create recipe stamp files. The path to an actual stamp file is constructed by evaluating this string and then appending additional information.

STAMPCLEAN

Specifies the base path used to create recipe stamp files. Unlike the STAMP variable, STAMPCLEAN can contain wildcards to match the range of files a clean operation should remove. BitBake uses a clean operation to remove any other stamps it should be removing when creating a new stamp.

SUMMARY

A short summary for the recipe, which is 72 characters or less.

SVNDIR

The directory in which files checked out of a Subversion system are stored.

T

T

Points to a directory were BitBake places temporary files, which consist mostly of task logs and scripts, when building a particular recipe.

TOPDIR

Points to the build directory. BitBake automatically sets this variable.

Appendix A. Hello World Example

A.1. BitBake Hello World

The simplest example commonly used to demonstrate any new programming language or tool is the "Hello World [http://en.wikipedia.org/wiki/Hello_world_program]" example. This appendix demonstrates, in tutorial form, Hello World within the context of BitBake. The tutorial describes how to create a new project and the applicable metadata files necessary to allow BitBake to build it.

A.2. Obtaining BitBake

See the "Obtaining BitBake" section for information on how to obtain BitBake. Once you have the source code on your machine, the BitBake directory appears as follows:

```
$ ls -al
total 100
drwxrwxr-x. 9 wmat wmat  4096 Jan 31 13:44 .
drwxrwxr-x. 3 wmat wmat  4096 Feb  4 10:45 ..
-rw-rw-r--. 1 wmat wmat   365 Nov 26 04:55 AUTHORS
drwxrwxr-x. 2 wmat wmat  4096 Nov 26 04:55 bin
drwxrwxr-x. 4 wmat wmat  4096 Jan 31 13:44 build
-rw-rw-r--. 1 wmat wmat 16501 Nov 26 04:55 ChangeLog
drwxrwxr-x. 2 wmat wmat  4096 Nov 26 04:55 classes
drwxrwxr-x. 2 wmat wmat  4096 Nov 26 04:55 conf
drwxrwxr-x. 3 wmat wmat  4096 Nov 26 04:55 contrib
-rw-rw-r--. 1 wmat wmat 17987 Nov 26 04:55 COPYING
drwxrwxr-x. 3 wmat wmat  4096 Nov 26 04:55 doc
-rw-rw-r--. 1 wmat wmat    69 Nov 26 04:55 .gitignore
-rw-rw-r--. 1 wmat wmat   849 Nov 26 04:55 HEADER
drwxrwxr-x. 5 wmat wmat  4096 Jan 31 13:44 lib
-rw-rw-r--. 1 wmat wmat   195 Nov 26 04:55 MANIFEST.in
-rw-rw-r--. 1 wmat wmat  2887 Nov 26 04:55 TODO
```

At this point, you should have BitBake cloned to a directory that matches the previous listing except for dates and user names.

A.3. Setting Up the BitBake Environment

First, you need to be sure that you can run BitBake. Set your working directory to where your local BitBake files are and run the following command:

```
$ ./bin/bitbake --version
BitBake Build Tool Core version 1.23.0, bitbake version 1.23.0
```

The console output tells you what version you are running.

The recommended method to run BitBake is from a directory of your choice. To be able to run BitBake from any directory, you need to add the executable binary to your binary to your shell's environment PATH variable. First, look at your current PATH variable by entering the following:

```
$ echo $PATH
```

Next, add the directory location for the BitBake binary to the PATH. Here is an example that adds the /home/scott-lenovo/bitbake/bin directory to the front of the PATH variable:

```
$ export PATH=/home/scott-lenovo/bitbake/bin:$PATH
```

You should now be able to enter the bitbake command from the command line while working from any directory.

A.4. The Hello World Example

The overall goal of this exercise is to build a complete "Hello World" example utilizing task and layer concepts. Because this is how modern projects such as OpenEmbedded and the Yocto Project utilize BitBake, the example provides an excellent starting point for understanding BitBake.

To help you understand how to use BitBake to build targets, the example starts with nothing but the bitbake command, which causes BitBake to fail and report problems. The example progresses by adding pieces to the build to eventually conclude with a working, minimal "Hello World" example.

While every attempt is made to explain what is happening during the example, the descriptions cannot cover everything. You can find further information throughout this manual. Also, you can actively participate in the http://lists.openembedded.org/mailman/listinfo/bitbake-devel discussion mailing list about the BitBake build tool.

Note

This example was inspired by and drew heavily from Mailing List post - The BitBake equivalent of "Hello, World!" [http://www.mail-archive.com/yocto@yoctoproject.org/msg09379.html].

As stated earlier, the goal of this example is to eventually compile "Hello World". However, it is unknown what BitBake needs and what you have to provide in order to achieve that goal. Recall that BitBake utilizes three types of metadata files: Configuration Files, Classes, and Recipes. But where do they go? How does BitBake find them? BitBake's error messaging helps you answer these types of questions and helps you better understand exactly what is going on.

Following is the complete "Hello World" example.

1. Create a Project Directory: First, set up a directory for the "Hello World" project. Here is how you can do so in your home directory:

```
$ mkdir ~/hello
$ cd ~/hello
```

This is the directory that BitBake will use to do all of its work. You can use this directory to keep all the metafiles needed by BitBake. Having a project directory is a good way to isolate your project.

2. Run Bitbake: At this point, you have nothing but a project directory. Run the bitbake command and see what it does:

```
$ bitbake
The BBPATH variable is not set and bitbake did not
find a conf/bblayers.conf file in the expected location.
Maybe you accidentally invoked bitbake from the wrong directory?
DEBUG: Removed the following variables from the environment:
GNOME_DESKTOP_SESSION_ID, XDG_CURRENT_DESKTOP,
GNOME_KEYRING_CONTROL, DISPLAY, SSH_AGENT_PID, LANG, no_proxy,
XDG_SESSION_PATH, XAUTHORITY, SESSION_MANAGER, SHLVL,
MANDATORY_PATH, COMPIZ_CONFIG_PROFILE, WINDOWID, EDITOR,
GPG_AGENT_INFO, SSH_AUTH_SOCK, GDMSESSION, GNOME_KEYRING_PID,
XDG_SEAT_PATH, XDG_CONFIG_DIRS, LESSOPEN, DBUS_SESSION_BUS_ADDRESS,
_, XDG_SESSION_COOKIE, DESKTOP_SESSION, LESSCLOSE, DEFAULTS_PATH,
UBUNTU_MENUPROXY, OLDPWD, XDG_DATA_DIRS, COLORTERM, LS_COLORS
```

The majority of this output is specific to environment variables that are not directly relevant to BitBake. However, the very first message regarding the BBPATH variable and the conf/bblayers.conf file is relevant.

When you run BitBake, it begins looking for metadata files. The BBPATH variable is what tells BitBake where to look for those files. BBPATH is not set and you need to set it. Without BBPATH, Bitbake cannot find any configuration files (.conf) or recipe files (.bb) at all. BitBake also cannot find the bitbake.conf file.

3. Setting BBPATH: For this example, you can set BBPATH in the same manner that you set PATH earlier in the appendix. You should realize, though, that it is much more flexible to set the BBPATH variable up in a configuration file for each project.

From your shell, enter the following commands to set and export the BBPATH variable:

```
$ BBPATH="projectdirectory"
$ export BBPATH
```

Use your actual project directory in the command. BitBake uses that directory to find the metadata it needs for your project.

Note

When specifying your project directory, do not use the tilde ("~") character as BitBake does not expand that character as the shell would.

4. Run Bitbake: Now that you have BBPATH defined, run the bitbake command again:

```
$ bitbake
ERROR: Traceback (most recent call last):
  File "/home/scott-lenovo/bitbake/lib/bb/cookerdata.py", line 163, in wrapped
    return func(fn, *args)
  File "/home/scott-lenovo/bitbake/lib/bb/cookerdata.py", line 173, in parse_config_fi
    return bb.parse.handle(fn, data, include)
  File "/home/scott-lenovo/bitbake/lib/bb/parse/__init__.py", line 99, in handle
    return h['handle'](fn, data, include)
  File "/home/scott-lenovo/bitbake/lib/bb/parse/parse_py/ConfHandler.py", line 120, in
    abs_fn = resolve_file(fn, data)
  File "/home/scott-lenovo/bitbake/lib/bb/parse/__init__.py", line 117, in resolve_fil
    raise IOError("file %s not found in %s" % (fn, bbpath))
IOError: file conf/bitbake.conf not found in /home/scott-lenovo/hello

ERROR: Unable to parse conf/bitbake.conf: file conf/bitbake.conf not found in /home/sc
```

This sample output shows that BitBake could not find the conf/bitbake.conf file in the project directory. This file is the first thing BitBake must find in order to build a target. And, since the project directory for this example is empty, you need to provide a conf/bitbake.conf file.

5. Creating conf/bitbake.conf: The conf/bitbake.conf includes a number of configuration variables BitBake uses for metadata and recipe files. For this example, you need to create the file in your project directory and define some key BitBake variables. For more information on the bitbake.conf, see http://git.openembedded.org/bitbake/tree/conf/bitbake.conf.

Use the following commands to create the conf directory in the project directory:

```
$ mkdir conf
```

From within the conf directory, use some editor to create the bitbake.conf so that it contains the following:

```
TMPDIR = "${TOPDIR}/tmp"
CACHE  = "${TMPDIR}/cache"
STAMP  = "${TMPDIR}/stamps"
```

71

```
T       = "${TMPDIR}/work"
B       = "${TMPDIR}"
```

The TMPDIR variable establishes a directory that BitBake uses for build output and intermediate files (other than the cached information used by the Setscene process. Here, the TMPDIR directory is set to hello/tmp.

Tip

You can always safely delete the tmp directory in order to rebuild a BitBake target. The build process creates the directory for you when you run BitBake.

For information about each of the other variables defined in this example, click on the links to take you to the definitions in the glossary.

6. Run Bitbake: After making sure that the conf/bitbake.conf file exists, you can run the bitbake command again:

```
$ bitbake
ERROR: Traceback (most recent call last):
  File "/home/scott-lenovo/bitbake/lib/bb/cookerdata.py", line 163, in wrapped
    return func(fn, *args)
  File "/home/scott-lenovo/bitbake/lib/bb/cookerdata.py", line 177, in _inherit
    bb.parse.BBHandler.inherit(bbclass, "configuration INHERITs", 0, data)
  File "/home/scott-lenovo/bitbake/lib/bb/parse/parse_py/BBHandler.py", line 92, in inherit
    include(fn, file, lineno, d, "inherit")
  File "/home/scott-lenovo/bitbake/lib/bb/parse/parse_py/ConfHandler.py", line 100, in include
    raise ParseError("Could not %(error_out)s file %(fn)s" % vars(), oldfn, lineno)
ParseError: ParseError in configuration INHERITs: Could not inherit file classes/base.bbclass

ERROR: Unable to parse base: ParseError in configuration INHERITs: Could not inherit file class
```

In the sample output, BitBake could not find the classes/base.bbclass file. You need to create that file next.

7. Creating classes/base.bbclass: BitBake uses class files to provide common code and functionality. The minimally required class for BitBake is the classes/base.bbclass file. The base class is implicitly inherited by every recipe. BitBake looks for the class in the classes directory of the project (i.e hello/classes in this example).

Create the classes directory as follows:

```
$ cd $HOME/hello
$ mkdir classes
```

Move to the classes directory and then create the base.bbclass file by inserting this single line:

```
addtask build
```

The minimal task that BitBake runs is the do_build task. This is all the example needs in order to build the project. Of course, the base.bbclass can have much more depending on which build environments BitBake is supporting.

8. Run Bitbake: After making sure that the classes/base.bbclass file exists, you can run the bitbake command again:

```
$ bitbake
Nothing to do.  Use 'bitbake world' to build everything, or run 'bitbake --help' for usage
```

BitBake is finally reporting no errors. However, you can see that it really does not have anything to do. You need to create a recipe that gives BitBake something to do.

9. Creating a Layer: While it is not really necessary for such a small example, it is good practice to create a layer in which to keep your code separate from the general metadata used by BitBake. Thus, this example creates and uses a layer called "mylayer".

Note

You can find additional information on layers at http://www.yoctoproject.org/docs/2.3/ bitbake-user-manual/bitbake-user-manual.html#layers.

Minimally, you need a recipe file and a layer configuration file in your layer. The configuration file needs to be in the conf directory inside the layer. Use these commands to set up the layer and the conf directory:

```
$ cd $HOME
$ mkdir mylayer
$ cd mylayer
$ mkdir conf
```

Move to the conf directory and create a layer.conf file that has the following:

```
BBPATH .= ":${LAYERDIR}"

BBFILES += "${LAYERDIR}/*.bb"

BBFILE_COLLECTIONS += "mylayer"
BBFILE_PATTERN_mylayer := "^${LAYERDIR_RE}/"
```

For information on these variables, click the links to go to the definitions in the glossary.

You need to create the recipe file next. Inside your layer at the top-level, use an editor and create a recipe file named printhello.bb that has the following:

```
DESCRIPTION = "Prints Hello World"
PN = 'printhello'
PV = '1'

python do_build() {
    bb.plain("********************");
    bb.plain("*                  *");
    bb.plain("*  Hello, World!   *");
    bb.plain("*                  *");
    bb.plain("********************");
}
```

The recipe file simply provides a description of the recipe, the name, version, and the do_build task, which prints out "Hello World" to the console. For more information on these variables, follow the links to the glossary.

10 Run Bitbake With a Target: Now that a BitBake target exists, run the command and provide that target:

```
$ cd $HOME/hello
$ bitbake printhello
ERROR: no recipe files to build, check your BBPATH and BBFILES?

Summary: There was 1 ERROR message shown, returning a non-zero exit code.
```

We have created the layer with the recipe and the layer configuration file but it still seems that BitBake cannot find the recipe. BitBake needs a `conf/bblayers.conf` that lists the layers for the project. Without this file, BitBake cannot find the recipe.

11 Creating `conf/bblayers.conf`: BitBake uses the `conf/bblayers.conf` file to locate layers needed for the project. This file must reside in the `conf` directory of the project (i.e. `hello/conf` for this example).

Set your working directory to the `hello/conf` directory and then create the `bblayers.conf` file so that it contains the following:

```
BBLAYERS ?= " \
  /home/<you>/mylayer \
  "
```

You need to provide your own information for you in the file.

12 Run Bitbake With a Target: Now that you have supplied the `bblayers.conf` file, run the `bitbake` command and provide the target:

```
$ bitbake printhello
Parsing recipes: 100% |###############################################################
Time: 00:00:00
Parsing of 1 .bb files complete (0 cached, 1 parsed). 1 targets, 0 skipped, 0 masked, 0 er
NOTE: Resolving any missing task queue dependencies
NOTE: Preparing RunQueue
NOTE: Executing RunQueue Tasks
********************
*                  *
*  Hello, World!   *
*                  *
********************
NOTE: Tasks Summary: Attempted 1 tasks of which 0 didn't need to be rerun and all succeede
```

BitBake finds the `printhello` recipe and successfully runs the task.

Note

After the first execution, re-running `bitbake printhello` again will not result in a BitBake run that prints the same console output. The reason for this is that the first time the `printhello.bb` recipe's `do_build` task executes successfully, BitBake writes a stamp file for the task. Thus, the next time you attempt to run the task using that same `bitbake` command, BitBake notices the stamp and therefore determines that the task does not need to be re-run. If you delete the `tmp` directory or run `bitbake -c clean printhello` and then re-run the build, the "Hello, World!" message will be printed again.

CPSIA information can be obtained
at www.ICGtesting.com
Printed in the USA
BVHW060618190521
607638BV00011B/1721